# The Bookcase....

## A collection of short stories

## by

### Robert Munroe

Soul Asylum
Poetry and Publishing Inc.

ISBN# 978-1-926876-23-8

Published in Canada by
Soul Asylum Poetry and Publishing
79 De La Salle Blvd, Jackson's Point, ON L0E 1L0
www.soulasylumpoetry.com

Soul Asylum
Poetry and Publishing Inc.

10 9 8 7 6 5 4 3 2 1

Project Editor: Kenneth Wm. Cowle, Charles Ross
Cover Design: Charles Ross

# Index

# *Foreword*

We are proud to be bringing you this first book by author Robert Munroe, of Sutton Ontario! A collection of short stories sure to grab you, and never let go! Rob has a unique way of gluing a reader to each story, hanging on to see how each life adventure will play out, and end! A very dramatic series of stories in this first collection, and just the beginning for this new writer to the Soul Asylum Publishing Label, as we are already working with Rob on his second collection of stories for publication, with a release slated for early 2012.

Make sure to keep your eyes posted for the next installment by this incredible story teller, and sit back and enjoy this gem!

Editor- Kenneth William Cowle

# Trick

October 31. Most of the leaves had fallen from the trees, calling to end a technicolour splendor. The temperature was hovering a few degrees above zero. Sunlight was at a premium late in the afternoon. One was already tired of winter, and it hadn't even begun yet. But, for the Kraggs, the most difficult aspect of this time of year was Halloween. You see, Mrs. Kragg was barren, and the couple were unable to issue forth offspring. Oh, what they'd give for wails and crying and googoos and spoiled diapers and music boxes and rattles and soothers and baby formula. Later on, they could envision reading bed time stories and Barbie's or Kens depending on their gender and their dream child. And then, before they knew it, there'd be help with homework, and then dancing lessons or hockey games. Then they'd be handing over the keys to the family car. And braces. Don't forget the possibility of braces.

The Kraggs remained a two person family. They had filled out tons of forms at the local adoption agency, but it appeared by the time their name came up, they'd be too old and tired to raise a child. There was more than enough love to go around after Sam and Rosie had hugged and kissed and shared in the events of their days. So they picked up the cutest and friendliest Black Lab at the local pound. Bartholemew. It was a delight to see his tail wag at din-din time, or to take him for a walk in the nearby park. The children would leap off the slides and swings and whirligigs and greet Bartholemew with a pat on the head or a rub on the soft spot underneath the ears. He would give a yelp of joy, and run with the children, chasing after the odd tennis ball. A dog's life isn't quite complete without a child to play with. Nor was a child's life quite complete without a faithful companion.

So Bartholemew was peppered with love by the Kraggs. And the Kraggs despaired over not having a child for the dog. But the dog was part of the family, and the Kraggs were enriched for having Bartholemew as a pet. Good doggie, they would whisper in the dog's ear, and Bartholemew would respond in kind, often giving Sam or Rosie a lick on the nose. The thought of having a baby in the house almost disappeared into the hidden recesses of their minds, but then Halloween would roll by. Who knows now where the ritual of All Hallows Eve originated from, or the term "Trick or Treat." It was a special time for children, when they could dress up as their favorite TV character or their dream hero. They would slip into a new identity and experiment with a growing realm of experiencing their core character possibilities. "Guess who I am," they'd demand, and the adult at the door would exclaim, "Oh, imagine having a visit from Cinderella, or possibly Frankenstein. " And Cinderella would curtsy, or Frankenstein would raise big arms and grown. Then they'd wait expectantly for a sucker or a mini chocolate bar or a pint sized bag of potato chips, and if they were offered an apple, they would turn their noses up and ask if there wasn't anything else they could be given. Then they would rattle their UNICEF boxes, and then go off with their booty in a plastic shopping bag, or with the bigger boys, a pillow case.

Children learn the best when they play. They stretch their imaginations and expand on their abilities when they shape and mold their view of the world and themselves. They are constantly discovering that there is more to them than they thought earlier. They also begin to differentiate between themselves and others, and begin to shape a singular identity. On Halloween, quite often, the little folk experience what Jung would call their shadow side, becoming ghosts or goblins or monsters.

They represent the darker side of mans soul, providing an outlet for aggressions or fears that are shunned by society, but will surface and magnify into horrific apparitions if not given a safety valve for release. So pumpkins are smashed and rolls of T.P. are unraveled and shouts and screams are uttered. All of this is rewarded by offerings of candy.

Sam worked as a Butcher at the local Loblaws. Rosie did the odd house cleaning for the neighbors. On Halloween morning, before Sam left for work, he threatened to wear home his bloodied apron and accompany it with a large meat cleaver. Rosie said that that would frighten the kids too much. It would be too realistic for Halloween. She reminded him to bring home some candy. Sam always bought the mini chocolate bars. Those are what he would like if he were a kid and out trick or treating. Each year he bought more candy than the year before, but this was more for his benefit, because for the three years they had been living in their present house, they had not had a single trick or treater knock at their door. They longed to have rabbits and penguins and ghosts and goblins arrive on their doorstep, but for some reason no one ever showed up. They entertained the thought of having little ones come to the door, as if the kids were their own. Was it because they were childless that no one came? Did their house appear haunted and scary? Or was it because they were situated at the far end of a short cul de sac? Regardless, Rosie reminded Sam to bring home some treats.

After Sam left for work, Rosie would take Bartholemew out for his morning constitutional, and then traverse the neighborhood to where the bigger houses were situated, and get down to vacuuming and dusting and polishing and waxing. She would join the mistress of the house for lunch and catch up on some rich gossip. She always saved the children's rooms for the last. She loved picking up toys and making little beds.

As she left, she would be paid cash, which she would place in a cookie jar on the kitchen window-sill. For emergencies Sam was the one who brought home the bacon, as he worked as Loblaws. The Kraggs consumed vast amounts of meat. Fat and cholesterol were their friends.

Sam arrived home carrying the groceries and a bag full of mini chocolate bars. He was wearing a "Torro" mask, his eyes peeping out from under the face cover. Rosie got a kick out of this. "Well, we finally got a trick or treater. I'll give you your treat later." Rosie went to get a bowl for the candy, and places it on the hall table. Then she went to work preparing dinner. She had a million and one recipes for red meat, so the two of them never got tired of their dinner fare.

Sam turned on the porch light and left the door ajar, hoping to attract visitors like moths to a light bulb. He decided to sample a candy bar. Rosie caught him and scolded him for having sweets before dinner. Sam said he would take Bartholemew out for a walk before dinner. Houses in the neighborhood were bathed in electric light, skeletons were pasted on doors, pumpkins with ominous smiles sat on steps, and one house had plastic ghosts hanging in nooses from a tree. It was already dark, but it was still too early to spot any costumes. Bartholemew ran ahead, his nose to the ground, on the trail of a particularly delectable scent. He did his business, and then returned to Sam's side. They both took a short cut home, eager to find dinner awaiting them.

Bartholemew was given his bowl of doggie chow right away, and then, with a full stomach, went to recline on the living room couch. Sam and Rosie sat down to a meal of steak pasta. They knew that Bartholemew would alert them to the arrival of any guests, so they concentrated on their meal.

While Sam was discussing what was on sale in the meat department and Rosie commenting on all the fun toys that little Johnny Crean had in his room. She couldn't help but pick up and push toy cars, manipulate the arms of tiny soldiers, or look out the window through a telescope. She was envious of Mrs. Crean, who had a child that she could smother with attention and love. If Rosie could have her way, she would give her child the best toys she could provide within her means. And she would be there to play with her child. But nature had squandered her dream. Hell, she would even settle for a nightmare. It would be better than having no child at all. She glanced through the living room, and saw Bartholemew, with his head resting on the arm of the couch. Thank god we're lucky to have such a companionable dog, always a friend, and so much a part of the family. A tail wag or a nose nuzzle can completely turn around a dreary day.

After dinner, Sam and Rosie joined Bartholemew in the living room, to watch their favorite game show on the television. Sam pleaded with Rosie if he could please just have one little candy, and Rosie laughed, saying that he should be sure to leave enough for the kids.

They waited and waited for kids to arrive, but the passage of three TV programs revealed no one. Sam was eyeing the candy bowl with anticipation... it was a good thing he bought extra candy this year. Bartholemew raised one sleepy eye lid, inspected the scene, and then went back to sleep.

After viewing a fourth program on the tube, Sam declared that, as in the past three years, they were to get no trick or treaters.

He went to turn off the porch light and shut the door, and grabbed the bowl of candy. As he sat down, Bartholemew raised his head and perked up his ears. He gave a short woof, followed by a full bark. There was a knock on the door. Sam looked at his watch. It was kind of late for children to come.

He rose out of his chair, and was followed by Bartholemew. He forgot the candy bowl. Standing at the door, waiting to be let into the hall, were four little cowboys. Complete with chaps and holsters and cowboy boots and black Stetson. With an exaggerated squeal of surprise, Sam exclaimed, "look what we have here, honey. Four desperadoes come to round up the spoils. Well, come on in and let me take a closer look at you." Bartholemew was sniffing one of the cowboys and wagging his tail, but the cowboy gave the dog a little shrug. Rosie came to the door with the candy bowl, to see if she could identify any of the kids. She was delighted to finally have a visitor on Halloween night after a blight of three years. They were all wearing masks, much like the one that Sam wore home from work. On closer examination, one had a very realistic looking beard, and the costumes looked like the real thing. They looked expensive. The first one through the door said "trick or treat" in what sounded like a mature, baritone voice.

Rosie held out the bowl of candy. One of the cowboys tossed the bowl onto the floor. "This is not a treat, this is a trick," he said, as the four pint sized cowboys pulled out their guns. Sam smiled, and said, "Very realistic. You look like real cowboys." "We are real cowboys. This is a robbery."

Sam laughed out loud. The gun of one of the cowboys was leveled at Sam's crotch. The three other cowboys barged into the living room. Rosie said, "I don't think these are your average trick or treaters, I think they're serious."

Robert Munroe

"You bet we're serious," said the cowboy with his gun aimed at Sam's crotch. Bartholemew was still sniffing and wagging his tail. Some guard dog! Sam and Rosie were shoved into the living room. The shoves had a fair force behind them.

"Hand over your wallet now," said the ringleader, "and honey, get your purse." Sam and Rosie tried to explain that they were of modest means and had little cash to hand over. The cowboys cocked their guns. Sam and Rosie handed over their cash. "Now, about your dowry, where are the family jewels?" Rosie started to cry. "Not my jewels," she murmured. "We're not leaving without them," said the ringleader. He handed an empty sock to Sam, and told him to empty all of their silver ware into the sack. Sam hesitated, and the cowboy assaulted him with the butt of his gun on Sam's knee. Sam reluctantly headed off to the dining room.

"Say, that looks like a new VCR," one of the cowboys piped in.

"Forget about the VCR. It's too big," said another. Rosie was followed up to the bedroom with a gun at her back. She shook her head in disbelief as she opened a drawer, lifted up some clothing, and revealed a small jewelry box. "Please don't do this to me," pleaded Rosie. The cowboy grabbed the box and stuffed it in his sack without examining the contents.

Back downstairs, the ringleader said, "Okay, so much for the tricks. Now how about the treats? Get me a nice cold one." "You're not serious."

The ringleader stuck a Marlborough cigarette in his mouth, and said, "got a light?"

Rosie descended from the bedroom, led by a gun at her back. "I've got the jewels. Now let's get out of here." said the cowboy.

8

"Why hurry," said the ringleader. "This is the only night of the year when we can actually get away with a heist and not worry about being caught. We can't be identified."

"There can't be many midget's in the area," pointed out Sam.

"Do you know who I am," said the cowboy.

"No, of course not."

"I'm just another little fry, a pipsqueak, a runt, a shrimp, a pee-wee, a gnome with a gun, a lilliputian. I could be a dwarf or a pygmy, but I'm not. What are the police going to do? Question everyone who's under four feet tall? No, we'll never be caught. Say, where's that beer?"

The cowboys settled into the living room, playing with Bartholemew and drinking beer and smoking joints. One raided the fridge, and upon finding it destitute of food, asked where the candy was. "Do you know what it's like to be a midget?" the ringleader asked Sam. Before Sam could answer, the cowboy continued. "Well, anyone over four feet tall just stares at you and backs away. It's a rare midget who is treated like an average person, given the lack of respect we get. No one takes a midget seriously. It is assumed that because we are small, we are childlike. Not so. The four of us got together as a gang to sort of prove that we are men. That we should be taken seriously and that we have declared war on big people"

"You know, for four years now, we have waited on Halloween to have kids frolic to our door and yell "trick or treat". We don't have any children of our own, so we crave contact with kids. And now you guys show up. You are hardly what we had hoped for. You come into our house and threaten us and shit all over our little sanctuary. It doesn't matter whether you're big or small, this isn't the decent think to do."

"What the Hell, its Halloween. The time when scary creatures surface from the wood works and peoples alter egos come out. We're just taking advantage of the time to conduct a little business. Gimme another beer. We're not finished here yet."

Sam and Rosie exchanged glances of disbelief and despair. Sam went to get the beer, and was relieved to find that it was the last one. One of the cowboys had rummaged through the house, and came back downstairs to claim that there was nothing else worth taking. "Let's hit the road."

The little cowboys rose from their chairs, belched and farted, and one guy urinated in the fireplace. They gathered their sacks, not as full as they had hoped, patted Bartholemew, and left cheering.

"Well, at least they didn't take all of the candy," said Sam.

"You and your candy. We've been robbed, for heaven's sake. We could have been killed."

"It's bad enough that my knee hurts from where the guy banged me with his gun. They won't get away with it though. I'll call the police right away"

Sam dialed 911, and reiterated to the dispatcher what had happened. The dispatcher said that the Tom Thumb gang had been quite active during the evening. The police were busy trying to trace their footsteps and apprehend them. She would send a cruiser over immediately. Meanwhile, she suggested that they make an inventory of everything that was taken.

Sam took Rosie in his arms, and Rosie burst into tears. 'It's not fair," she managed to squeak in between sobs. "The only trick or treaters we get in four years turn out to be pint sized thugs." Bartholemew came and sat beside the couple, looking up at them with sorrowful eyes. He then pawed Sam's leg.

Robert Munroe

# My Friend

## MY FRIEND, LOVELY TO SEE YOU...AGAIN!

There comes a time in everyone's life when they come to a fork in the road that is their life. The fork that diverges to the west is filled with dreams. I'm going to be a world famous flautist...James Gallway will ask to open up for me. Or, perhaps I will be a world famous artist, on par with Pablo Picasso or Vincent Van Gogh. Or I will write a best seller and be on the New York Times best seller list for years, soaking up royalty payments that will amount to millions of dollars. Then again, why make a choice? Why not be a Renaissance man and dabble in all of the arts? The only problem with looking at life this way is that very few people have the patience, discipline or motivation to endure the lengthy apprenticeship that is necessary in order to reach a level of ability that is recognized as a satisfactory level of achievement, something that one could live off of for their time left on this earth. There is also the puzzle of skill or aptitude; do I really have what it takes to make it as a creative soul? Most of the time you can't know for sure until you have given the practice of art your very best...lots of time and effort.

If you come to the crossroads and take the east fork, you end up with the necessities of life only. Work from nine to five in a job where you never know if you'll have a job to go back to the next day. Buy a car and a house in the suburbs and spend a large allotment of time paying off mortgages and car payments. Fit in the rat race and keep up with the Jones's, living in a world where the imagination lights up when there is something new to consume. Banality, conformity and a lackluster spirit hardly inspire one to look elsewhere for sustenance...you end up in a socially accepted rut and anything that diverges from this path is seen as threatening and unwelcome.

A person usually reaches the fork in their road in their late teens or early twenties. You can guess the route I chose by the pin-striped suit and my Docks shoes. I thought that when I had a nest-egg of savings I could always retrace my steps and see what the western fork would hold for me, except it doesn't work that way. Once you start making money, your needs grow proportionately, and your youthful dreams take second fiddle to appearances that you must keep up. So here I am, working in an upper office in the Bank of Montreal building, busting my ass for a corporation that wants to bleed me as dry as a stone. The more work you do, the more there is to do, and it is more expected of you than appreciated. It is a vicious circle that never abates.

Every so often, to escape the protocol required of you by the downtown business core, I take a walk up Young Street from King Street to Bloor. Despite the fact that the grand old lady of streets, the longest in the world and 200 years old, changes as you head north on it, Young Street still has a palpable feel to it. Around King Street, one is dwarfed by skyscrapers and swallowed up by business people exuding wealth. The Eaton Centre is a sheltered temple where people go to be part of a crowd and ogle at spectacular displays and layouts of merchandise the stores claim we all need. North of Dundas Street, there are strip joints that we are assured that we can purchase the illusion of sexual gratification for the price of a beer and a table dance. Heading north from loudspeakers suggesting that all virile men should come in and have a look and fulfill their fantasies are, huge record stores, stereo shops and t-shirt palaces. Every so often I have to take a walk up Young Street to help put into perspective where I spend my time working and why I do so.

Despite its age, Young Street really isn't a young street. Fast food restaurants, heavy metal bars, army surplus stores and clothing stores showing off in the latest fashion trends, all combine to appeal to young people on the move, with all the time in the world. There is a sense of urgency to the street. The loudspeakers, neon signs and window displays all contribute to the feeling that one can achieve Nirvana instantly by partaking in what the street has to offer.

I escape from the hustle and bustle of King and Bay Streets by walking up Young. There is a sense of dirt and grime and sleaze on the sidewalk. It could be called Sex, Drugs and Rock & Roll Street. There is a blatancy to how we can get what we want...as if the street and stores were the embodiment of a mass libido that is bubbling just below the façade we present as to what is acceptable. King and Bay Streets are likely a finely tuned Ferrari engine that propels a fast and efficient car that knows where it is going. Young Street on the other hand, is like a pig wallowing in his own shit. It is caught up in the frenzy of self indulgence of the ever-present NOW. Every so often I need to go back to the pig-pen that is Young Street, to be caught up in the immediacy of fulfilling ones baser tendencies. It is sort of like the soldiers who would head for Vietnam to Hong Kong for rest, relaxation and restoration of the soul. Once you have let go and immersed yourself in something completely different from your status-quo, then you can go back to the rigid and stultifying ways of your daily routine, feeling a little lighter and less distracted after satisfying basic urges that would grow out of proportion if not satisfied every so often.

Up Young Street I would march, stopping into the sleaziest bar I could find, then go to one of the major record conglomerates and pick out the latest in punk rock, and buy a pair of cowboy boots that would be more at home in a prairie farmers field than in the business district of Toronto.

I would flow through hoards of street youths, hookers who would claim they were "tight," drunks and derelicts and the dispossessed. Even if I were rich, I wouldn't have enough money for all of the panhandlers that would single me out. I would see Mohawk hairstyles, full leather gear, brand name t-shirts and jackets. There would be eyes of oblivion glancing at me, as well as eyes of anger. Every other store would proclaim that they were having a sale, jockeying into position for the money of the young who have yet to be weighed down by financial responsibility. My world on King Street was going places, quarterly reports and profits and five year plans were carefully developed for growth. On Young Street, one forgets the past and the future and aims for the satisfaction of the moment. In a way, I go to the strip to forget. We all have something to forget every now and then.

The busiest time of year in my business world is the summer. At this time, one prepares marketing, advertising and promotional scenarios for the new fall season. For a little while, I'd be putting in eighteen hour days, trying to work out the best sales strategy to sell our product. One afternoon, on a late August day, I just had to get away for a couple of hours. I was running out of steam from the immense pressure of trying to orchestrate a plan to get new items off the ground and into the hands of the public. I feigned illness (only half true…I was sick of the work), and took the afternoon off. I sought the distractions of the strip.

I broke the momentum that long days slaving over sales figures and projections provide, and started walking north. The heat, haze and mugginess of the afternoon served to reinforce the jolts of bright lights, sound bites and the smell of urine and jostling with the crowds that was taking place all around me. Those who weren't lost, wished they were.

I soon forget the numbers I had been chasing after for the past few weeks, and became an observer, taking in my surroundings as if I were Sherlock Holmes. However, I was not prepared for what I encountered outside an instant teller machine way up around Wellesley.

Unlike the beggars and hustlers and the hopelessly inadequate street musicians I had encountered on my way up the strip, here was the genuine, original, 100% musician. He had on The Who t-shirt and torn jeans, the uniform of the musically inclined, but was not just another street busker. He had the appearance of youth, but looked old enough that he knew what he was doing. He had his guitar case laying open in front of him, with a spattering of coins in it, but he seemed not to notice, so immersed was he in his music. He was dancing with his fingers up and down the shaft of a 12 string acoustic guitar, bringing out the magic of the music that was locked inside the instrument. After the conspicuousness of the lower part of the street, the music from this guitarist bathed in sincerity, softness and delicacy that made the serenade from this musician stand out to my delight. I stood against a store front and listened to a couple of songs before continuing on my pilgrimage up the strip. The musician hardly noticed I was standing there, listening. Just as I was about to take a step, my friend started in on an old Moody Blues tune. The one that goes, "Lovely to see you again, my friend."

I was studying in California at the time that this song was a mega hit. I liked all of the Moody Blues songs, but this particular tune was one of my favorites. At the time, it was blasting from stereos, I would listen to it with my friend Carmellita.

It was one of her favorites too. Carmellita and I would get involved with different worlds, but we would always meet again after a period of time and space away from each other. We would greet the others by saying, "Lovely to see you again, my friend." It was like the pillar or foundation that united us again after being apart. It was the signature song of our relationship. The relationship existed only in my imagination after Carmellitas car went out of control and smashed into a highway light standard. I lost my friend just over two years ago. Listening to the Moody Blues song became impossible. My feelings of anger and loss and frustration were too much to bear witness to. I wanted to run away, anywhere away from the song, but decided to stay and hear out the piece. Tears started to well up in my eyes, and a hand over my mouth muted quiet sobs. The musician suddenly became aware of my presence, and said, with soft humor, "I didn't know I was that bad a player." I briefly explained the hiatus I had taken from the song, and he said, "The Moody's are tops in my books, and I particularly like the same song you do." I nodded in acknowledging his comment, took a twenty from my wallet, and dropped it in his case. I started walking, amazed at the multitude of associations one song can carry with itself.

The afternoon of hockey away from work did me a world of good. After taking time out to see how the rest of the world lives, I was able to set back into some productive work with my figures. Hearing the song that Carmellita and I held in common, regardless of boundaries of time and space between us, was cathartic. It brought back feelings that had long been held submerged from my conscious mind. It's such a small thing, hearing a street musician play a song, but what repercussions.

Work slowed down as fall approached, and soon I felt like slumming again. Young Street is like a witch's cauldron. You add a bit of forbidden this, and prohibited that, and you end up with a potion that wakens you to thoughts, feelings and instincts that you think better not to explore, but the concoction actually energizes you by recognizing what actually lies within you, me, and everyone else, but are usually too afraid to look directly in the eyes at. I saw and took in everything on the street, from the worst to the best. As I approached Wellesley, I thought I saw the young musician who had so touched me with his rendering of the Moody's song. It looked like he was encouraging passers-by to deposit change in the Styrofoam cup he so carefully cradled. At one point he retrieved a cigarette butt discarded by a pedestrian. The great guitar maestro had been reduced to begging for small change and recycled butts. I watched for a while as people out for a walk would rebuke him and hold his pleas in contempt. There is a lot of desperation on the strip, but it didn't sit well with someone who had touched me so deeply.

"What in the world are you doing," I asked. "What happened with your guitar?"
"It's a long story. Believe me, I wouldn't be begging and banging butts if I didn't have to."
"You enchanted me with your playing. Let me guess, business wasn't going so good, so you pawned your guitar. Am I right?"

Actually, it was stolen. I went for a quick nip, and next thing I know, I'm waking up on a park bench, with no guitar in sight. It was really my own fault. I know better than to indulge in Jack Daniels. It goes down so smoothly, especially after singing on the street. I tell you, I learned my lesson. Never again will I go drinking with my guitar in tow. A booze-up like that is just too expensive."

"You helped me tremendously by unearthing and exposing feelings I had long since forgotten. Every experience in ones life is important, whether it be delightful or horrifying. They are all parts of us, and we don't do ourselves a favor by remembering some and forgetting others. Look, I give hundreds of dollars a year to the United Way, and when the Daily Bread Food Bank has its food drives, I chip in and help them, too. It seems to me that you've fallen on hard times too, although you're not entirely innocent in your undoing." I fished in my wallet. "Here are two "C" notes. You should be playing, not begging. Take care." And I was off. You don't really recognize disparity in others until it impinges on your world in some way. Then you have to take action.

As Fall passed and it got colder, work slowed, too. I was putting in 8 or 9 hour days, a far cry from the super human efforts of the summer and early fall. I was still following a good momentum, but I wasn't nearly as restless, and I didn't feel any great need for escape. But I still had to pay tribute to my baser instincts sometimes, and for this I would take a stroll up Young Street. There were the usual desperate people to whom a couple of bucks would send them into flights of ecstasy. There were others from which anything could be bought or sold as if in a commodities market. There were furthermore those who didn't care one way or another. The ones without hope would join the homeless, sick and mentally ill from the winter before who succumbed to the elements and became statistics in the Chief Coroner's reports. The homeless should spend the winter in Miami, not Toronto. Young Street transforms virgin snow into dark, muddy slush...not conductive to outdoor habitation. I wondered how my favorite street musician was doing.

I spotted him at his usual location, outside an instant teller machine at Wellesley and Young Streets. He was only minimally dressed for the elements, wearing an open bomber jacket over a t-shirt. As I stood across the street and observed him, he seemed more concerned with bringing his guitar to life than any acknowledgement in the form of money that might come his way. The look on his face told me he was living completely in the world of music, frets and struts replacing any concern for food or drink or cigarettes. At least I thought so. When he seemed to finish one song, he reached into his bomber jacket, pulled out a brown paper bag, and blessed his lips with some form of nectar. Ten to one odds, it was his best friend and worst enemy combined, Jack Daniels. I was about to cross the street and confront him about the dangerous mix of alcohol and his guitar...was he really considering the repercussion of his actions. After giving him the money to replace his guitar, I kind of had a vested interest in making sure he kept on strumming. He also touched me like no other concert hall diva could, because of his wonderful ability to render the beautiful sound of the Moody Blues. I stopped myself when I saw what must have been another musical compatriot approach my friend. The other figure seemed much worse in stature. He too, revealed a brown paper bag, and offered my friend a drink. After sharing slaps on their backs, the two headed south.

It was really none of my business...as long as people don't hurt each other or impede me in my pursuit of my goals, I don't really care what other people do. Nevertheless, I followed the duo to the parkette just off the main drag. I stood inconspicuously behind a crop of hedge and observed the newcomer take a sip of whatever was in the brown bag. Then he would pass it to my friend, who would reciprocate with three or four sips. In no time, my friend has started to slouch and slither somewhat on the bench.

When it became obvious that my friend could no longer respond to or react to his surroundings, the newcomer left his bottle on the bench beside my friend and proceeded to walk away with the guitar my friend had purchased with my charitable donation. I was about to confront the thief, but a number of punkers came by, and after raising some high fives, they left...with the guitar. I went over to see if there was any way I could help my friend, but he was so far gone in an alcoholic haze that the only thing I could do was to leave be to sleep off his intoxication.

The next day I walked up to Wellesley again. I didn't do it to escape the world of King and Bay Streets, nor to make contact with my baser self. I merely wanted to make sure my friend was alright. Sure enough, there he was with a Styrofoam cup, asking everyone who passed for some loose change. He hungrily eyed anyone who happened to be smoking. I asked him where his guitar was. He said that it went with his last sip of Jack Daniels. "That's two guitars that you've lost to Achilles Heel...that's about $400.00. You don't look like you could afford another one right now." He replied, "Actually, that's the eleventh guitar that I've lost in the last little while. They seem to be disappearing faster than ever. I'm getting good at negotiating with the pawn shop brokers. Even still, they make a lot of money off me."

I proceeded to tell my friend about the little bit of surveillance I had done the day before. He said that he didn't really know the guy he drank with...he had seen him once in a while in one or more of the bars my friend frequented. "Look, it's becoming obvious to me that as a street musician, people in the neighborhood are familiar with who you are. They also seem to be aware of your drinking habits.

They know that if they invest twenty or so odd dollars on J.D. and offer it to you, you'll gladly accept, and knowing that you have no limits, save passing out completely, when you drink, they'll walk off with one of your guitars and earn a healthy profit. Think about it for a while. People are taking advantage of your weakness for booze.

"Are you telling me that there is a conspiracy among my drinking buddies to rid me of my guitars?"

"I think your friends can read you like a book, and know how to pull your strings to their advantage. If you must drink to celebrate a good day busking, take your guitar home first, or consider drinking at home. How will you buy a new guitar? I'm not in the mood to give you more money for another guitar that you'll promptly lose."

"Actually, I'll get an FBA cheque at the end of the month."
"That's still fifteen days away. That's a long time to go without hearing The Moody's."

"Well, things seem to have a habit of working out in the end. No need to worry."

At that I gave my friend a playful punch on the shoulder and wished him luck, warning him to take heed of where and who he drank with. I swam down to the morass and muck of Young Street to my office.

On the second day of the new month, I made a hike to Wellesley again, delighted to find that my friend was sporting another twelve string acoustic guitar. He was so wrapped up in singing and playing that he didn't realize that I was standing there watching him. Every nerve and fibre of his body was consumed by his music. He noticed me after a few minutes, and promptly switched to Carmellita's and my song by the Moody's that had so affected me earlier. Once again I took out my wallet and rewarded my friend with a twenty dollar bill. Things seemed to be on the right track again.

As December advanced, and cold, biting winds mixed with snow and slush and ice, I made the trip up to Wellesley less frequently. On one occasion, I could see there was going to be trouble...he was swaying to the music more than usual, and his encyclopedic memory of song lyrics was interspersed with "yahoos." When he spotted me approaching him, he yelled, "Hey, man, lets you and me go for a couple shots of J.D." If I joined him, I'd have a lot of catching up to do. I reminded him of his tendency to lose guitars when he went drinking, and he responded by giving me his guitar. "I don't trust myself when I drink, but I do trust you. After all, you have been my most generous fan." He left me with his guitar and staggered up the street, yelling, "make that a triple J.D." even before he entered the doors of the bar.

When I arrived back at the office, numerous people commented on the fact that I was carrying a guitar. "So you're going to moonlight as a guitarist?" they'd say, or "you're planning a career change, are you?" I took the guitar out of the case, and made a few futile efforts to strum music. I told them the truth...I was merely holding it for a friend for a day or two while he was "out of town." And I did return to Wellesley a couple of days later. I approached my friend with the words, "My friend, lovely to see you...again." He smiled and took the guitar, immediately breaking out in the song that meant so much to Carmellita and me. He wasn't just playing for me and my memories of Carmellita though. He was so immersed in his music, it was obvious that he was playing for himself, and if his very survival depended on a pick striking a string.

I never saw my nameless friend again. He had talked about joining a band, or moving to Vancouver, where the weather is more bearable in the winter. Wherever he went, I knew his guitar would be right by his side, and hopefully he wouldn't lose it over a drunken binge.

It was clear to me that when we reached the fork in the road, I turned east while he turned west. On the surface, it appeared that I had made the "right" choice, but when I consider the divergent paths our lives took, I'm not so sure. My friend had the courage to follow his dream. He was totally involved in his music. Maybe one day he would be a big rock star. But I don't think that possibility was a big concern for him. He lived for his music. In contrast, I took the easy way out. I had money, some semblance of job security, and a daily routine I could hide behind. However, I never took a risk. My dreams were just that...dreams. My friend lived life passionately. Me, I had a job to attend to, day by day. I did it out of a sense of obligation to accumulate wealth, not because I wanted to.

Robert Munroe

# Granny Napping

It wasn't as if he were as regular as clockwork, in fact, far from it. Days would go by, even sometimes weeks or months, before I would hear from Rambling Raymond. And at that time I would get the collect call, it was as if we had talked just hours previously. Maybe he had been panning for gold in the Yukon. Maybe it was a diamond mine in Sierra Leone. Maybe it was the Gorillas in Rwanda, or Pygmies in Ghurkas in Africa or Nepal. Sometimes it was something as simple as a rainbow, or as difficult and extreme as a Forest Fighter in Northern Alberta. Entering war zones was like the proverbial piece of cake. He could disguise himself in any manner of clothing to get into areas not usually welcoming to the Western World.

His idol was Gaugan, an executive that gave up everything he had in order to paint Polynesian beauties in the Pacific Ocean. The seed was there even when I knew him in late Elementary School, where he would devour bare-breasted women and startling geographic scenes in National Geographic Magazine. He would camp and ride his bike for endless miles as if exploring, and make forts in trees to keep out of reach of enemy fire. He would read up on remote locales such as Antarctica or Pictairn Island, and read first hand accounts from explorers such as Marco Polo, Christopher Columbus, Stanley and Livingston and Sir Richard Francis Burton. By the time he graduated from Elementary School, he had already traversed the world many times in his imagination. A High School trip to Paris, France just served to whet his Wanderlust. The only problem was that travel cost money, so he ended up (for the time being) on Bay Street in Toronto's Business District as a Junior Executive, with the potential to save up enough money to hit the open road.

Rambling Ray had a difficult time working on Bay Street, where every penny counts and accuracy is everything, numbers just weren't as exotic as a trip to Fiji. His Mother and Father and brothers all accused him of having too many dreams in his head and not enough in the way of plans down on paper. His family was distressed that, no matter what he did, or how he did it, he was as much as a non-conformist as one could be. There are social protocols and business regulations that he was blind to or was completely ignoring and claimed oblivious to. Most people didn't know what to make of him and were, in a world of number crunching and conforming to get to the top. They were a little fearful of this free spirit.

It wasn't that we were the best of friends or anything... sometimes we would bump into each other on Bay Street and have lunch together. If opposites attract, well, ours was the epitome of that. He was always a bit aggressive in his dealings, whereas I didn't want to rock the boat on my way to the top. We would talk about common friends and what they were doing, and Ray would say, "if only I had enough money to...", but that was still to come. We had both studied business, hoping to make it big, but Rambling Ray seemed more interested in saving up to DO something, rather than make an investment in his future (and any family that may eventually come). I was socking as much money as I could into RRSP funds.

One day I received a call from Ray. He said he had to see me right away. I figured he wanted to talk about another impossible dream of his. I thought, why not? Raymond was interesting if sometimes aggravating.

So I agreed to meet the next day at the Timbuktoo Room. I didn't know what to expect. But then, I never knew what to make of Ray. When I met him, he was sitting with a pint of Guiness and a twinkle in his eye. "Rob", he said, "it's time to blow this popsicle joint and spread my wings in this great big world of ours." He was looking at me with a combination of familiar reminiscences and future anticipation. "I'm leaving for Coober Pedy next week." I was puzzled but not completely surprised. "Where in the world is Coober Pedy and why would you want to leave your family?" "Coober Pedy is an opal mining town in the middle of Australia. It is so hot and so remote that people live like moles underneath the earth's surface." "Why there and why now," I asked. "I read an article in National Geographic many years ago, and it seemed to me to be one of the most exotic and unusual places in the world. My Granny always encouraged me to see the rest of the world while I could…my parents and brothers live in Granny's house, but she's starting to be a bit decrepit, so I thought I should take her up on her advice. After that I'll try and get a job on one of those vast Australian Ranches."

It was easy enough, of course, to see where Rambling Raymond was given his moniker. Tourists have destinations, whereas many travelers (outside of businessman) travel in order to keep some desirable state in perpetual motion. With Raymond, it was his Grandmother who paved the way for Raymond's development.

I always think that each succeeding generation is the exact opposite of the preceding one.

That is because of the learning process that is passed along from each generation. We learn from others' mistakes and grow through others' successes. And if someone tries diligently to force you in a particular destination, it is pretty well a given that youth will rebel and deliberately choose an opposing direction to follow.

Raymond's Granny welcomed him, his parents and his brothers into her large house as she grew older and her faculties started to deteriorate substantially. She would enthrall Raymond with all of the time zones and all of the latitudes and longitudes she had traversed. If there was an account of someone's travels being published, there was a good chance she had been there before them. She had been through countries that were now inaccessible due to politics, war or famine. She had hobnobbed with the rich and famous, with saints and sinners, politicians and Clergy. She had spent time in Paris in the 20's, dancing with Nijinski, painting with Picasso, having invitations to visit Gertrude Stein in her salon, and modeled for Rodin. She was one of the first to settle down with a copy of James Joyce's Ulysses. But times changed and so did her desire to move on.

During the Second Great War, she spent time in Britain and Switzerland as a Translator and Spy, and worked in an Ammunitions Factory. She put her heart fully into these pursuits, for to her, she would do anything for the war effort, and always liked to immerse herself completely in whatever she was doing.

# Black Bile Saga

I could feel the black bile slowly cursing through my veins as slow and dark as molasses. I myself reacted in kind. My response time and general strolling ability was about on par with a tortoise. Who would think that my life would come to this, I asked myself as I peered over the bridge abutment and envisioned myself leaping over the edge and splashing and splintering into a kaleidoscope of pieces as I hit ground zero.

Every terminal case, when facing the barrels of a firing squad is supposedly granted one last wish. Unfortunately, dying a death by old age, letting nature pass the sentence, mountain clogged arteries and an irregular heartbeat, and wrinkles as deep as the grand canyon, had been met with great guffaws. No, what was meant was a last feast of steak and eggs, a kiss from a loved one, interspersed with trembling and tears, or at least one last smoke. My last wish was to escape from this prison of emotions and feelings and thoughts. But I also brought along a Century Sam cigar. I felt that one's last smoke should be fitting of the occasion.

So there I was, glancing into the darkness that was to become my fate. I was sucking on my cigar, wheezing and hacking, feeling faint and probably turning blue. Maybe this wasn't the King of last wishes, but I felt that I had to mark my last minutes and seconds with a desperate token, a cigar, a big fat corona stogie. After each puff, I would watch the incendiary tip crawl and creep towards my index and middle digits, indicating my time left on this dreary and depressing veil of an earth. The burden of being Jack Kirk had become a wheelbarrow of garden stones, an automobile with an unwelcome rattle and a shoe with an ever present pebble in it.

A TV screen with a blur of static. Each and every difficulty that had stuck to my back was surmountable as individual entities, but when they all came at once and stuck to my being like crazy glue, well, I was just about finished with my cigar.

I slowly lifted my right leg onto the wall of the bridge, much like a dog taking a leak after being kept indoors all day. I reminded myself that I was afraid of heights, but that my purge of limbs would be quick and certain.
"Son, you don't want a permanent solution to a temporary problem, do you?"

I glanced around to see an immense bear of an officer approach slowly, has cruiser door left open, befitting the state of emergency that I had declared.
"There's nothing that can't be worked out, no matter how bad things are."

I shifted my frame until my crotch was being crushed and smothered under the weight of my frame. I wanted a reprieve of another couple of moments before I leapt over to the far side of darkness, but the presence of this officer had expedited my decision to descend into oblivion.

"What's your name?"

"Jack. And don't come any closer. I'm going to jump."

"Jack, you don't want to jump. Things have a way of turning themselves around."

"I guess in your line of work, you get to experience the dregs of humanity, the lost causes and the black hearts. Don't ccme any closer." I shifted my weight to let my balls breathe a little better. "Well, my whole life is in shambles. I have been repatriated to hell. Unfortunately, I can't go back to my life as it was."

"Then you have to look to the future, to take a new stance towards life."

"Fuck you. I have no hope left for the future. Things just won't work out. The fates have dealt me a hand without fingers. Make it easier on yourself. Don't look."

The officer had inched himself closer to me. I thought I could smell garlic. It was now or never. I swung my leg right over the edge, and as I straddled the barrier, separating me in hell from a peaceful, if empty oblivion, the officer rushed me and pulled me off my perilous vantage point, with a quick grab at my left shoulder. I was dislocated both physically and mentally.

As the officer had me on the ground, he cuffed my hands behind my back in one swift, skilled move, helped me up, and led me to the cruiser. He slid me on to the back seat, shut the door ominously, climbed into the car, and picked up his walkie talkie. In lingo that was as fathomable to me as the bottom of the ocean, he communicated with a superior, then turned to me through the mesh barricade and said he was going to take me to the hospital.

It was about a ten minute trip through sparsely travelled streets to get to the destination. Instead of treating me like a fugitive or bounty, he asked me what I thought about the Leafs, and whether I had ever been to Florida (he goes down every February to escape from the blanket of snow on the ground, and the wind chills that seep through down filled jackets.

The figure who had so rapidly pirouetted with my destiny was obviously familiar with the emergency department at the hospital.

Even though the hospital had been dispatched regarding my arrival, after registering at admittance, the two of us sat immobile in a sparsely appointed waiting room, surrounded by cries and screams and wails and concerned relatives and intravenous hook ups. Patience proved to be a herculean effort as we waited for the psychiatrist to show on the scene. The officer offered me a stick of gum, talked about the unknown quantity that was the Raptors, and piled me with questions about myself. I was mute. After three hours of despairing for my immediate future, the Psychiatrist arrived, more questions that I couldn't rise to. I could taste the black bile on the tip of my tongue. With a signature inscribed in stone on the forms in his hands, I was admitted. The officer who had been like a sentry to me, wished me all the best, and said that with professional help things would begin to look more rosy. Two porters arrived shortly after, and as I was hustled up to the seventh floor, I heard over a voice implanted in the ceiling, "Porters STAT to seven west." I started to think "escape."

The jaws of the elevator opened, and I set foot on virgin ground. We passed the front lobby, where three people were watching television with glazed eyes. The nurse's station was like a beehive with nurses filling out charts and making calls and soothing teary eyes patients. Occasionally a chilling scream would drift through the air, and a nurse would bolt from the nurse's station. I expected to see disembodies souls, but all I saw were people pacing the floor, with faces drawn taught. The porters handed me over to my nurse, Ruth Ellen, and I was led to room 767. Close enough to the station that they could keep an eye on me.

I felt like a stranger in a strange land. I was checked for anything that might contribute to me harming myself, and issued hospital garb. I was placed on close observation, which meant that I was stuck in limbo. Ruth Ellen asked me why I wanted to disown my life, and all that I could muster was the unadulterated fact that my life was over. She took my blood pressure, and waited until the thermometer was removed from the underside of my tongue before asking me if there was anyone who should know where I had been deposited.

I started to cry at this point, her question laden with hopeless and helpless expectations. She patted me on my sore shoulder to console me, and said that things would get better, they always do. I just had to be a patient patient. She introduced me to the rituals of the floor... meal times, groups I was expected to attend, where the linen was kept, and the joys of the pantry late into the night. I would see my psychiatrist for a brief consultation every morning, and she or other nurses on duty would be there for me if I was having difficulties. She then left briefly to get me my prescribed medication. Before I consumed it and it slunk down my throat, I asked what it was and what it was for. Prozac. Say I'd heard of that before. Trailing it was a fistful of controversy. Wonder drug on one hand that enhanced black market consumers, and a sure footed road to aggravated insanity on the other hand. I hesitantly downed the green and white capsule, hoping to travel down the median of the road.

Ruth Ellen left, a promise on her lips that she was available if I needed any help. I lay back on my bed, pondering the chains that bound me to the world of the psychologically bereft

I could feel the black bile oozing out of every pore. Why hadn't I been a little more resolved with my balancing act over the bridge, and why had life intervened in the form of a cop? As I lay there, I could feel the heaviness of slumber descend on me, and I jumped off the abyss of wakefulness.

I was wrestled awake by a figure standing over me with a clipboard in his hands. "Mr. Kirk? My name is Dr. Amin. I am the Staff Psychologist. Mondays through Thursdays I hold a psychology group in the music room. It is an informal gathering where I talk about various concerns, and share comments and questions with the patients. It starts in five minutes." Seeing a face of fear in front of him, he asked if this was my first visit to a Psychiatric facility. When I nodded, he said, "left talk about it in the group." A trial of compassion and understanding followed him out of the room.

I groped my way down to the music room, still feeling a bit groggy from my snooze. I sat down in an empty chair, and rather cautiously glanced around the room. Seated within the room was a mixed group of men and women, some in pajamas and some in street clothes. Legs stretched out or curled up underneath bottoms betrayed concerns etched onto the array of faces present.

Dr. Amin entered the room, clipboard and mug of coffee in hand, and shut the door. He eased himself into a chair, took a swig of coffee, and began marking hieroglyphics on his clipboard.

"I never know what I'm going to talk about until I sit down and see my group. A psychologist is different than a psychiatrist. A psychiatrist makes diagnoses and prescribes the appropriate medication. I can't prescribe drugs. My job is to talk and listen, to make solid and sculpt the concerns and feelings and ambiguities inherent in the experiences you are undergoing at the moment. Your Psychiatrist deals with chemical imbalances and genetic abnormalities. I try and put your situations in perspective. It is kind of like six of one and a half a dozen of the other. Our brain matter dictates to and guides us in how we feel. But it is also considered true that our outlook on life, our ability to face and deal with carious stresses and burdens can affect our body chemistry. So your psychiatrist and I sort of work a tandem. Finding the right medication that works for you is important, and medication can be the fastest route to mental health, but to have deep and lasting results, you need to come to terms with your life. Talking out of a depression can take a long time. After all, you didn't get sick overnight. And often there are several factors contributing to your illness. I may have the solution to your problems, but it is not like I am offering you a canapé on a silver platter.

No, the issues troubling you have to be looked at from every angle, held up to the light to identify cracks. Upon exploration, we often don't see the situation for what it is, at first glance. It has to be mulled over and considered like a chocolate covered peanut, layer upon layer melting until we come to the core matter. Two aspects of illness that come to mind are repressed anger and lofty expectations. Some of us were taught by our parents that to express our emotions, particularly the more volatile ones, is unacceptable. If we are constantly placed in the position of being punished for expressing anger and the like, we turn these emotions in on ourselves. We become depressed. The emotions we experience are real, almost solid. They reach the surface in one way or another. They won't just disappear into thin air. It is important that in expressing buried anger, that it be done in an accepting environment. That is where I come into the picture. By having help recognizing and sorting out your deepest, darkest anger, you take some of the wind off of its sails. It becomes one of many emotions you feel, and is no longer so threatening to yourself. It is directed appropriately outwards, and the more you come to realize this, the more benign its effect will be on you."

I glanced from Dr. Amin to the rest of the group. One person had drifted off, and was breathing heavily. Others nodded and seemed keen to hear the Dr. explicate further. One person got up and left the room, claiming thirst, but she never came back. In the far corner was a guy who had wrapped himself in a bed sheet. His eyes darted back and forth between Dr. Amin and the rest of us. He had fear written across his face, and appeared that he was about to tremble like a Richter 6.3 quake. Dr. Amin was lulling me with his comments. He seemed to know what he was talking about, although I didn't feel like much of this applied to me. But I was willing to listen some more.

"Another contributing factor to your difficulties, and I find this to be the case more often than not, is that you have too high expectations for yourself. We are only human. Superman exists only in the comics and movies, fictional all the way. But too often we set our aims too high, as if we were some kind of superhuman creature. By doing this, we only set ourselves up for disappointment.

For there is only so much we can do, and no amount of wishing or hoping or planning or plotting can change the basic reality that we are human and thus are limited in what we can achieve."

"I don't have high expectations, but I still feel discouraged. I can't seem to bring myself to do the things that I usually get pleasure from," said a woman sitting on the couch.
"When you are depressed, everything slows down. It becomes a major effort to feed and cleanse yourself, and it becomes harder and harder to carry on your social and occupational relationships. You have to reduce your expectations further down the notch. When you begin to feel better, then you will be able to cope better with your obligations. You can't run when you've got a broken leg. It's the same thing with depression. You can't expect to do the things you usually do with the same fervor."

Black bile, I thought.

"Let's see who we have here...Mr. Kirk...what brings you into the hospital?"

"I'd rather not say," I replied hesitantly.

"Well, think about it. It usually helps to lay your cards out in the open. Then you can examine the results and attempt to make some sense of it all. I should remind everyone that anything said in this room is to be kept confidential. Mrs. Quarry, you've been here before. Explain to Mr. Kirk the process."

"Well, I am manic-depressive. It is a chronic ailment that comes and goes. My life is like a roller coaster. I have highs, and then I dip to stomach turning lows. But I eventually snap out of it. If you're sick, then the hospital is the place for you. You'll find that you have much in common with the other patients. Me

I'm mad at the world for the way it treats me, and I'm furious at myself. I feel like such a loser and a failure. Right now these feelings are overwhelming me, but in the back of my mind, I know it isn't true. Things will turn around."

"That's fine for you to say. But as for me, there's nothing out of balance. I am a failure, and nothing any Dr. or nurse will do will make any difference to me. My life is over."

Dr. Amin questioned me. "You said that this is your first visit to a psychiatric unit. Have you been given a diagnosis yet?" "Yes, Black Bile it is so far."

"What do you mean by Black Bile?"

"I used to be called Midas, as in King Midas, the fellow of ancient Greek fame. Everything he touched turned to gold. Nothing could go wrong for me. Just like that old king, everything I did turned out to be ten times better than expected. Then, overnight, all of my precious metal turned to dust. And the way things have gone, there is possibility of salvaging anything from the past. My mind and body have turned into a stinking mass of putrefying, rotting, and festering Black Bile."

"So, you're depressed."

"Depressed isn't the right word for it, it's more like ruined. I have lost everything, most importantly my self- respect. I am now wandering through this world of ours as if blind. I have lost my rudder as well as a sense of direction. I tell you, I'm finished."

"Tell us what happened." I was always tops in school, and graduated cum laud. I joined a small business that showed every possibility of skyrocketing in business volume. I married my high school sweetheart once my future was secured.

I managed to put a down payment on a house, and proceeded to get children and dogs, which were kept from straying with a white picket fence. Then came an opportunity to beat all others. My boss wanted to make me a partner in the business. All I needed was a substantial amount of cash. Luckily, the bank saw the almost no risk possibilities of this small company just beginning to poke its tiny eyes above the horizon. Well it was a con job. My boss took off at a crucial moment, with my money and enough loopholes that I would never see my money again. I don't know how I wasn't able to see through the scheme. Due to my blind spot and because of my association with the enormous swindle, no one would hire me. I couldn't keep up with my house payments, my wife and child gave up on me in dismay, and left. I was forced to find a shabby apartment. Fortunately, I had the unconditional love of Fido, but he was run over by a car in a singular moment of freedom from his leash during a walk one night. Then, one day an auditor from Revenue Canada knocked on the door. I knew my troubles had just begun at this point. All this has nothing to do with depression. I am tainted with Black Bile. There's nothing that can be done. That's when I headed for the bridge.

"It certainly sounds like you've had your share of bad luck. There have been a lot of difficult changes in your life over a condensed period of time. Change is always stressful, whether it be positive or negative. There are many things in your life that are irretrievable, but their degree of severity will decrease over time. New opportunities will arise, and you will be able to examine them through the lens of experiences past.""No, I'm not a lost cause, an athlete past his prime. Things won't get better, they'll just get worse, although I can't see how right now." I looked around the room to see how the other patients were taking this.I could tell that they had been listening to my every word, giving me a non-judgmental ear, but whether they identified with my confession, I couldn't tell. "Memory works in a strange way. Right now, you are in the middle of a series of bad experiences. Just the thought of these things drains all of your time and energy. But your memory is selective. It doesn't remember the pleasurable and comfortable things, countless hundreds or thousands of little things that would have given a small lift to your day in the past. An accurate memory would balance the scales, not tip it to the depressing side. In the long run, things are rarely all good or all bad. It is the way we focus our attention to our memories and tend to them that makes us feel out of whack. Revenue Canada isn't going to banish you to Tuktoyuktuk. You won't always live in a dingy rooming house. You may be reunited with your family when the dust settles, and if not, there are other women out there. And there are dozens of loving and devoted dogs waiting at the pound to find a new home."

"No one would want me right now. The passing of time may alleviate some of my pain, but the wind has been knocked out of me. Things will never be the same again; I'm finished."

"You will have a tough time of it for a while, but eventually you will be able to gain an accurate perspective on your life. Then the pain and anger and frustration will loosen its grip on you. Your Black Bile will be a thing of the past. Try and think of something that you have enjoyed doing in the past that you could look forward to doing when you are discharged."

Just then, a nurse poked her head in the room, her eyes settling on me. She wrote something on her clipboard, and exited as suddenly as she entered.

Robert Munroe

"Well, I have family who own property up at Lake Simcoe. I used to enjoy going up there for mini family reunions every so often. I would gather up my loonies and put up the "out to lunch" sign and..."

"Who are you calling loonie? And I'm not out to lunch." (this from the bed sheet in the corner). Dr. Amin just gave me an encouraging glance to continue.
"When a number of us gathered up there at the same time, it was crazy. It was pure bedlam with the younger fry and the dogs." Don't call me crazy. I am not crazy," said the bed sheet in the corner.

"Mr. Kirk is not referring to you, Mr. Boyle. He is merely using generic terms to describe what his visits were like." I didn't know if this was sinking in to Mr. Boyle. His eyes were darting back and forth over the faces of everyone, pausing for an extra second when he found my face. I can remember getting up in the early hours of the day and sitting with Gramps at the kitchen table, having my favorite breakfast in the whole world...a sliced banana on a bowl of fruit loops."

"Bananas...so that's what you think of me. And I take offense to your usage of the term "Fruit Loops."

"Please," I pleaded. "I am not referring to you in any manner. In fact, your barely distinguishable underneath that bed sheet of yours."

"Just leave me alone. Cut me out of it," demanded Mr. Boyle.

"Mr. Boyle is suffering from paranoid delusions. He thinks everything and everybody is referring to him. Rest assured, Mr. Boyle, that no one means to upset you. Please continue Mr. Kirk."

"One of my favorite things was to play marbles with my cousin Ralphie. One visit though, I lost my marbles, so Ralphie shared his with me." I should have known... "lost my marbles." Mr. Boyle immediately claimed that he had a full head of marbles, and to quit insinuating otherwise.

"Before the big Sunday dinner, the adults would gather around with drinks in their hands, and I would raid the trays of cheese and crackers, and bowls overflowing with nuts. It was a great time."

"I think you're crackers," interrupted Mr. Boyle. "And you can have those nuts."

"Take it easy, Mr. Boyle. Mr. Kirk is referring to food, not your state of mind. Just relax. No one here thinks badly of you. You were saying, Mr. Kirk?"

"Well, there was an apple orchard not far away from the family homestead. In the fall, when the apples had ripened and matured, I would go up and do some picking, pausing to eat the odd fruit. But because I was only a pipsqueak, I couldn't lift a full load, so I was always a few apples short of a barrel by the time I called it quits and dragged my booty to the car. I really enjoyed…"

"I beg your pardon," interjected Mr. Boyle. "I am not missing any apples. My barrel is overflowing. Don't mince words with me." I was beginning to fathom what life was going to be like on the seventh floor, co-existing with basket-cases of varying degrees. Needless to say, I didn't utter the term basket-case out loud, neither did I mention that, while on a picnic, by the time I came back from a short hike, the picnic hamper was one slice short of making a sandwich. Nor did I mention the time we were out on a boat cruise, and found a screw loose in the hold. Fast thinking on my part with dads screw driver saved the boat from becoming engulfed with water.

And I didn't mention that I drove Rover around the bend by throwing his ball off the wall until he was completely out of breath. And of course, all of my endearing labels given to my cousins such as daft or mad or certifiable or wacko stayed out of hearing in the deep recesses of my mind. I could see Dr. Amins point about memory being selective. I enjoyed remembering my visits up to the lake, regardless of what Mr. Boyle made out of them. But in my present situation, I didn't think it would have any extensive result. Another patient shared her views on selective memory, and Mr. Boyle was prepared to slay more imaginary dragons breathing fire at him.

Dr. Amins attention shifted to other patients with other concerns. I had planned just to listen while in his group, but I was actually thankful for the chance to open up and reveal parts of myself. And in the group setting, I realizes that I wasn't the only who's life engine had seized up on them. Mr. Boyle appeared to be the most difficult or extreme case of madness on the floor, but I soon came to the conclusion that he was harmless. When Dr. Amin said, "Well let us stop here for today," I thought that maybe this wasn't the wrong place for me after all, although doubts kept on surfacing now and then. I went over to thank the Dr. as he got up to leave. He said that he would talk more during tomorrow's group.

I slipped silently and effortlessly into the routing on the floor, attending then groups with as much eagerness as lunch or dinner. I made a number of friends, and I was amazed at how mental illness infiltrates all borders of sex, race, religion or age, brilliant or semi retarded. And I felt a sort of relief and peacefulness being away from all of my concerns and wrapped in the warm cocoon that was the seventh floor.

My problems didn't disappear on me. Instead I began to see them as added pebbles in the stream of life. The nurses and my psychiatrist began to comment that I was looking better long before I felt a noticeable change in myself. But it was true. A combination of time and medication and therapy restored my strength, and my faith in myself grew. The Black Bile that had so immersed me in its powers eventually thinned, and was replaced with a healthy flow of blood. My selective memory became such that I had a firm grip on many joyous moments, and the image of me perched on the bridge became fuzzy and distant.

When I left the hospital, none of my family or friends or acquaintances ever called me Midas again. That suited me just fine. I was satisfied with Jack Kirk.

Robert Munroe

# Jada In Haiti

I was turning 9 years old, it was my birthday. Me and mama had been to the market and that she was we bought some yams and some apple juice. When we came home, mama said going to Auntie Delia's house and she would be right back. I was sitting in our little kitchen at the table and I was drawing mama a picture. All of a sudden everything was moving and shaking and there was terrible noises coming from every direction. I wanted to scream but no sound would come out of my mouth. The chair I sat on began jumping and sliding so I got off and got down on the floor and grabbed the table leg and held on tight. I could hear myself screaming in my mind; MAMA, MAMA, MAMA, over and over again. The shaking went on and on and everything was coming down from the walls and then it looked like the walls themselves were falling. I wanted to crawl to the door but I could not move. There were groaning sounds coming from above me and the ceiling was moving closer to the floor. I finally screamed out loud and squeezed my eyes shut tight. Suddenly there was dust and dirt and all the white plaster on the walls floating around in the air. Something fell on the other end of the table and two of the legs broke. I stayed under the little space the table made while the walls and ceiling continued to close in on me. I wondered when this horrible shaking and noise would stop, it seemed like it had been going on forever now.

All of a sudden the shaking stopped and then it was very quiet. I was in a darker place than I had ever been in before the shaking started and there was very little space around me. I blinked my eyes because there was so much dust on them. I felt around me and felt my arms and legs. Nothing seemed to hurt but mostly I could just feel my heart pounding and my chest hurting from breathing in the dust.

I began to cry. It just seemed to start up all by itself and suddenly I was wailing with all my strength and I screamed for mama. I wanted her to come and get me right now and tell me that everything was going to be alright. I felt so afraid and alone...

After a little while I stopped crying and I just sat in the little dark space. I strained to listen for any sounds that I could hear. I wanted to hear mama coming to get me out of here. Where was mama? When would she come? She knows I'm here I thought to myself. I could feel myself wanting to cry again but this time I wouldn't let myself cry. I wanted to show mama how brave I was when she came to get me.

I am nine years old now I thought. And I am brave and I am strong I told myself. We are going to have my birthday party today and mama said Auntie Delia and all of my cousins were going to come and celebrate with us. I knew that my mama had gotten me a new dress but she didn't know that I knew. She wanted to surprise me but I had seen it at Auntie Delia's because I had walked into her tiny house and found her sewing it. She was taking up the hem and adding shiny new ribbons to it. So I said to Aunty, "Oh, what a beautiful dress Aunty. I would like to have a wonderful dress like that." Aunty had looked at me funny and said, "What you doing coming in here and scaring me like that Jada girl?" I saw the smile in her eye and I smiled at her and put my hands on my hips. "I like to scare you Aunty because your eyes go big!" I said as I laughed. "Not as big as yours when you looked at this here dress, sassy Jada." she had replied as she reached out to hug me. I loved Aunty Delia because she played with me and told me stories about our family and my Daddy and what a sassy girl my mama had been when she was a little girl.

Aunty Delia had five children and she and Uncle Jerome worked very hard to look after all of them. Uncle Jerome worked six days a week in the downtown area and aunty took in washing and sewing. Every Sunday, mama and I would o to their house and together all nine of us would go to the big cathedral where we prayed to god and sang songs and laughed and joked with the other people who came to church. The priest would tell us of our history when he talked about how God had helped the slaves of Haiti to free themselves and how our little country in the Caribbean would become the promised land God had promised us. He told us to be strong, have faith in God and persevere because we were close to seeing the promise come true. I loved going to the cathedral with me family. We were happy to be together and afterward we would picnic near the big presidential palace.

Thinking of aunty and mama, I began to wonder if they had felt all the shaking that I had felt. I wondered if they knew that the house had fallen down and I was still in it. I looked through the murky light and really looked at what was all around me. There were chunks of the wall in piles all around me and pieces of broken wood and all our cups and plates were smashed in pieces everywhere. I looked out from under the table and could see that the roof of the house completely covered the whole mess and that there was no was out up there. As soon as I thought the words "way out" I could feel my heart start pounding hard again because I realized that there was no door anymore. Or windows. I felt like I was going to panic and frantically try to push everything out of my way to let me get outside. I want out of here, I thought. I want out. I want out. I want out. My mind wouldn't stop screaming.

Suddenly I heard something. People were shouting and screaming out there. Some of the screams were terrifying, like the people who were screaming had seen the devil. I began screaming too. "Help me! Help me! Mama, mama, mama!" I screamed. I began moving around in my little space, trying to find room to stand up in. I pushed against the stuff that surrounded me and found that it wouldn't budge. Everything seemed to be locked tight and I began to feel like I would suffocate. It became very hard to breathe and I just wanted to cry again. Instead I began to pray and asked God to help me get out of there. I pleaded with God to bring my mama to me. I wanted to be safe in her arms and feel her strength and love.

The noises outside seemed constant now and I listened to hear voices that I recognized. Where was all my family? My mama and aunty and all my cousins? Where was uncle Jerome? I decided to lay still and quiet until I heard them coming to get me. I wrapped myself around the table leg and shifted around until I got in a position I could rest in.

Today had been such a beautiful day. I went to the missionary school in the morning and me and mama had spent the afternoon walking through the market. She had teased me about being a big, grown-up girl and asked me did I think I might someday marry a rich man? We laughed but I began to think about becoming a woman and what I would find in the future. Life seemed to be getting a little easier lately, with the missionaries visiting us regularly and bringing us food and books and clothes. Mama worked at the mission several days a week cooking big meals for all the staff and the children and she would bring home dinner for us on those days.

I really liked going to school because the teachers promised that if we got a good education we would be helping to turn our country into a good place to live. I thought about the day that the beautiful woman who lived in Canada had come to our school. She was from our country and yet she had gone to this wonderful place and become the Governor General. Boy did that ever sound important. And she had beautiful hair and makeup and the most glorious clothes. She talked to us and hugged us and encouraged us to be good students and aim high. I remember deciding that day that I wanted to be just like her when I grew up. At school I studied hard and helped the teacher with the younger children. I wanted to please that beautiful Governor General Lady and I wanted to please my mama.

I must have fallen asleep because suddenly I woke up. I lay very still and brought my hands up to my eyes because I couldn't see anything. It was very, very dark. The noises from outside seemed to be coming from very far away. The screaming had become quieter but the shouting went on. It sounded like people calling out for each other, searching and listening for family members. I sat up as tall as I could and I yelled, "I'm in here, please help me! I can't get out!" I tried very hard not to be afraid in the darkness. I tried to think of the lovely birthday cake my mama had made for me. I felt really bad that it was here in this kitchen with me and I had not even tasted it. We were going to share it with everybody and I would get the last and the biggest piece. That is the way we did things in our family. I realized that I was hungry, my belly gurgled and hurt me in that funny way that hunger does.

I was lucky not to be hungry very much because I knew that some of our neighbors didn't have work and so many times they were hungry. Mama's job and the mission made sure that I always had something to eat.

Why has nobody come for me? It has to have been hours since the great shaking. It must be night time now, it is so dark. I am so scared and I feel so alone. Where is mama? What happened to her when the great shaking came? Is she still at auntie Delia's? Oh mama, I need you so bad mama.

I sat still in the darkness and I wondered how I would know how much time was going by. When would morning come? Surely they would come and get me out of here tomorrow. I will walk, I told myself. I will walk and I will find mama and auntie and we will build a new house. When we have that new house we will have a party with lots of food and some soda pop. Suddenly I realized that I was very, very thirsty. I need to have a drink of water. Where will I find water? I knew that there was a pail of water on the sideboard before the shaking. Was it still there? What about the apple juice we had bought? Oh, that was a special treat for my birthday party. It was on top of the table when the shaking started. Was it near? Could I reach it? I felt around me in the dark and tried to squeeze around to the back of the table. I kept reaching around, thinking the juice was in a plastic jug and maybe it was not broken. Something made a sloshy sound and I knew it was the juice and my hands frantically flew around searching for it. I must find it. I need to drink something. My mouth is parched from dust and I've had nothing for hours.

My hand came upon something that didn't feel like broken wood or smashed crockery. It was a yam we had bought in the market

I felt a sudden surge of joy like there was light inside me. I could reach the yam and it would make my belly feel better and maybe take away my thirst. That little yam felt like hope to me. I felt a strong certainty that somebody would come and find me and mamma and me would be together again.

I wiped all the dust and dirt off the yam with my skirt and then I brought it to my mouth. I gnawed some of the skin away then just held the yam to my mouth and sucked at it, imagining the thin juice as water that gushed forth.

Eventually, after I had slept and woken up once more, it began to get a little brighter where I was. I realized that I could see light coming from the outside. I strained my eyes to see how the light was getting in because I began to hope that maybe I could find myself a way out. I was going to get out. Maybe my mama needed me and that's why she didn't come. I was going to get out and help my mama. I suddenly felt a surge of strength and energy and I started crawling over the rubble towards the light. I began to chant to myself, "I am coming to you mama. I am coming to you mama." I just kept saying it over and over, especially when I found my way blocked. I thought of mama and her beautiful smile and the way she sang at church and how in charge she was at the big mission kitchen. I thought that I will put on my new dress and me and mama will go to the mission. They will take us in when they find out our house fell down. I will live with the orphan children and go to school with them and we will be happy.

I kept slowly crawling and squeezing my way towards the light. I gathered dust in my hair and got many scratches on my arms and legs but I kept going towards that light. Mama will be so happy when she sees me. She will laugh at my dusty head and tell me I need a bath. And I will have a big drink of water…and I will live.

Robert Munroe

# The Seventh Surprise

It was love at first sight. No, no scratch that. Crumple the page and sink a two pointer in the waste basket. It's too much of a cliche, and not entirely true. There certainly was an initial attraction, i would like to think, from both parties.

Perhaps it is more apt to say that she was a fashion plate. Again, a bit cliched, but perhaps more to the truth. She was "a long drink of water," clearly clocking in at about six feet. Her hair was the colour and consistency of scrambled eggs, her eyes the deep blue and sweetness of a lollypop, her lips as if she had just bitten into a ripe, juicy strawberry, breasts that could provide a rich, thick, milkshake, a bottom the shape of a pear pulled freshly from it's branch, and thighs like the fluted stem of a tall wine glass. Yes, plate is a better word to describe her. Her high cheekbones would fetch a premium price at the butcher shop if she were ever to be slaughtered.

Every so often there would be a neighbourhood get-to-gether. We would all agree to meet at the Marrian's of the Swigton's, great libations and conope's being served. We were an exclusive neighbourhood, and these occasional parties would allow us to keep up on the news of Dan's new career move, or little Jimmy's latest coup in the minor hockey league. Basically, we were reminding ourselves that we had made it, so to speak, and we each took turns recognizing and supporting our lastest accomplishments. Usually it was a small, closed circle of neighbours that gathered, but on the occasion in mind, the Wintellas brought along a guest, a cousin from frigid Winnipeg, who had arrived in the relatively balmy Toronto winter. As I mentioned, she stood out in a gathering already known to be exclusive, intelligent and successful.

At the time of this particular gathering, i was twenty seven years old, and a victim of my own success. I was an accountant who had made it. I had a large house in an exclusive neighbourhood, a Rolls Royce in the garage, and twenty hour days sometimes, servicing a very wealthy clientelle, many of them my neighbours. But the house sat empty for most of the day, and despite a twenty minute commute to work, the Rolls sat in the driveway, or in an underground parking lot downtown by my office. I had no time for a wife, a dog, a child or a white picket fence. I focussed all my energies on work, trying to travel between rich and richer.

It was thus quite a surprise when i met Marnie McMillan, guest of the Wintellas, at the home of the Sampsons. I was supposedly the most unavailable of available bachelors in the nieghbourhood, and I figured my reputation had proceeded me to the party. Marnie asked what I wanted to drink as she approached me. To my reply of GinTonic, she went to the fully stocked bar in the basement, ad returned with a generous, cool, frosty glass of my heart's desire. She peirced my eyes with a glance of her own blue babies, and i had to ask, "is there something wrong?" "I am gifted with the ability to look into peoples souls by looking into their eyes. After all, the eyes are known as the mirrors to the soul." "What do you see in my eyes?" I asked.

Her gaze was so piercing and persistent that i wanted to shield my eyes, but let her magic work, as i would come to recognize it.

She paused for a few seconds, walking through my eyes into

my soul, before she commented. " You are an Aires, stubborn and strong, an overachiever, and are not fearful of doing anything that will further your career and increase your wealth. You are a bachelor, fearful of making a commitment that would eventually devour you and suck the lifeblood out of you like a leach. There will soon be a change to your life that will take you by surprise. A social change, nothing to do with your work. In fact, I can see seven major surprises in your life. You can be ruthless in your work, but these surprises will serve to make you more human."

I didn't really make anything about the surprise, let alone seven of them, but she was bang on about the rest. I was too distraught by the fact that once a woman knows you are a man of means, they get all lovey-dovey and they can't wait to become attached, only to take your credit card and financially bleed you dry, and then they  want to live in the lap of luxury, you providing everything and them taking everything, never satisfied, and then they divorce you and expect half of your estate in the process. The first thing I noticed about Marnie was that she was a provider. She got me my drink, and was very stimulating in her physique and her fortune telling. She was to big, she had such a presence, that i knew she would not be a taker. That was my particular mind reading stint.

We chatted for a little while, and then she left relatively early with her relations, but not before she gazed further into my eyes, and then directed a backwards glance to me as she left. I had an image of her magnificent stature and her strong, powerful,directed and insightful gaze that would creep into the TV screen of my mind at certain times of the day or night.

It was shortly after that that she returned to the arctic ice bucket that is know as Winnipeg. It wasn't long after that i received a letter from Marnie, via my neighbours the Wintrellas. In it she said that she had suffered to many unbearable winters in Winnipeg, and wanted to escape from the clutches of her family. She was coming to Toronto, and was wondering if I could take some time off to show her around the town. Well, i certainly wanted to feast my eyes on this Amazonian once more, and i had been working incredibly long hours at the office, so I thought I deserved some time off. "Certainly," I wrote, "I'd be glad to give you a guided tour of my fair city." The only thing to add was, "when are you planning to arrive?"

She arrived shortly after, taking as little time as possible to wrap up business in Winnipeg. She moved in with her relatives the Wintrellas, and was eager to spend an evening on the town with me.I took her out to dinner at the Imperial Room at The Royal York Hotel, where her unusual habit of peering intensely into peoples eyes unnerved me at first, then we went to The Colonial Tavern, at the time one of the most prestigious and important Jazz club's in the city, if not the country. Then I managed to get us into the observation deck of what at the time was the tallest building in the commonwealth, The Canadian Imperial Bank of Canada Tower.

Nothing escaped the fiery glaze of those beautiful blue eyes, which certainly gave my hormones a rough and bumpy ride. she said she knew i would be dressed in pin stripe blue, that i would drive a conservative, expensive car, and even suggested the rack of lamb as i was about to order the very item on the menu. What she couldn't see through those prophetic eyes, she would quiz me. To her, Toronto was another world, and would ply me with questions while trying to comprehend what was done, or what existed in my city. After a wonderful evening out, I drove her to the Wintrellas, but she did not get out of my buggy until i had tasted those strawberry coloured pair of lips, and laid my hands on those wonderful mounds of breasts. Keep in mind that I had sublimated any kind of relationship or sex life into my work, so that this wonderful exploration of Marnie's assets had all that more impact on me. Her enthusiastic questions and curiosity brought out thoughts and feelings that I thought I had done away with long ago.

It wasn't long before I was calling up Marnie every night... She would bring over an apple pie (you guessed it; my favorite) or a sweater or casual shirt (again, my favorite colour). She gave herself with no hesitation, and i was a very willing recipient. It was something I didn't recognize at first, but there was no doubt I was falling in love.

One night we were sitting in front of my fireplace, the fire crackling and providing much welcomed heat, having liquors after a wonderful chicken pasta, when i mentioned to Marnie that I was experiencing strong emotions towards her that I thought I was immune to. "I know," she said. "What else do you know?" I inquired. She had a grin that lifted one side of her mouth with bemusement, stared again into my eyes, and said, "I will soon be your wife." I smiled somewhat shyly, nodded my head in agreement, and said, "I never thought it would be possible to agree with such a statement, but I'm afraid you're right."

"I've know right from the very first time I laid eyes upon you, that we were ment to spend our golden years together, not forgetting some hot and heavy times between now and then."

"You did, did you?" my upturned lip showing some amusement with the comment.

"When I first met you, i could see that we would share seven surprising turns in our lives together. The first is that we would become husband and wife."

"You knew that right from the beginning?"

"It was the first of seven surprises i could see. But it wouldn't have done any good to bring this to your attention on our first meeting... you wouldn't have been ready to accept or understand the situation."

"Well, what about the other six surprises? Can you give me any clue as to what else will follow?"

"I knew from the time my penetrating eyes rested on yours that we would be ment for each other. As for the other six surprises , I can't be sure. All i know is that there will be seven altogether. Of that I have no doubt."

I had no doubt, either. Her perceptions were so accurate, there would be more surprises guaranteed. And the few things that escaped her eyes, she would fill in the blanks with astute questions. This ability virtually rendered one the need to spill one's guts and share every detail, thought and feeling one possessed. And with more queries, her eyes became all that more knowing.

We wasted no time in attending to the need of our nuptials. It would be held in Winnipeg in May, with her family and a select few friends of hers and mine. Several of my friends in both work and play were astounded that Marnie and I were to tie the knot. If it was destined, so be it. And why waste any time (except waiting for Winnipeg to warm up) when our hearts and minds were one on the matter.

We took the train from Toronto to Winnipeg, to make somewhat of a holiday out of the trip, complete with the bulging suitcase filled with formal wear and other things appropriate for such a trip. We had our own private compartment on the train, but spent most of our time in the dinning car, ordering only the fanciest of dishes, and copious quantities of alcoholic beverages. Or we would ride in the scenic car, the one with the dome of glass, so that we could gaze onto the great vast spaces, the pre-cambrian rock formations, forests dense with newly budding trees, or pass through little Hamlets were a train passing through was a big event, and mothers and children would stand at crossings and wave greetings at the passing travellers.

Marnie stayed at her parents' home while i booked into the Red River Inn. one of the premiere hotels in Winnipeg. Over the course of a few days, I learned that Mr.McMilan was a Supreme Court of Manitoba Justice, that her mother had been a suffragette before just about anyone else had ever uttered such a word, and that one brother was studying law and the other was just about to graduate as a mechanical engineer. Altogether an impressive family, but with all of the abundance of achievements in her family, Marnie, with her insights and questions about virtually anything was by far the most captivating of her family.

The wedding went well, Marnie looking pristine and fresh and so beautiful in her wedding gown, and I was so enamored by the sight of her that I wanted to kiss the bride before saying "I DO" and being granted the " You may kiss the bride" by the minister. There was a small reception after the wedding service, followed by a dinner at a mens club Mr. McMillan was a member of. It was a small gathering but i welcomed the opportunity to meet her parents and brothers and a few select friends. The reception went late, when Marnie and i retired to the bridal suite at the inn, and spent all night carefully inspecting and teasing and consummating our wedding night, becoming familiar with each and every pleasure center, bump, curve, mole, bruise, scent, until we had full carnal knowledge of each other. Needless to say, we didn't get much sleep that night, and although we had a "Do Not Disturb" sign on our door, I'm certain no chamber-maid would have ventured into our suite without seeing that we had checked out in the first place.

The next morning, or should i be realistic and say, "much later in the day," we thanked everyone for their wedding presents (each one held a particular meaning for the particular gift bearer), the wedding itself and the wonderful reception after, gave our farewell kisses and waves, and headed to the airport for our honeymoon in Quebec City.

For our honeymoon we made the Chateau Frontenac our home, taking horse and buggies through the old walled city, eating in well known and century old restaurants, walking hand in hand through farmers' markets, outdoor art shows, watching street magicians, mime artist musicians, finding incredibly old, quaint and fascinating neigbourhoods, and shopping in some of the finest and most exclusive shops anywhere. We were so generous to ourselves and each other that we had to pay a visit to the luggage merchandiser to carry home our additional purchases. It was a whirlwind week, were we saw and did so many things that such a city has to offer. It was difficult, at the end of two weeks, when it was time to return home, to face the fact that rarified experiences we had shared in such a special time and place and was about to end. How long would it be before our lives and and relationship to each other become common and mundane?

Upon arriving back in Toronto, we unpacked our honeymoon mementoes, and tried to make home a "sweet" home. Marnie had several cheats of cloths and other essentials that had arrived from Winnipeg, and was busy unpacking and rediscovering many things she might not have had use for before, but were necessary as a newlywed and housewife. My house on park lane was large and imposing, wood paneled walls, a mammoth fireplace, a kitchen with every appliance you could think of for the time, a canopy bed and huge walk in closet, and a book lined study. However since i worked incredibly long hours, the house had none of that lived in feel that a proper home should have. It was almost as if it was one of those haunted houses that you see in movies, cloth covering the furniture as if it was a cocoon, huge spider webs, curtains drawn, dark and dusty and musty rooms, no air circulating and the only room alive was my study, to which i would retire after an excruciatingly long day, only to put in a couple more hours of work before getting to bed.

When I first met Marnie at the neighbourhood party, and shortly afterwards we would spend much of our time together out in the town, with only a couple evening spent at the house (now our house), so she was aware of my living wuarters and my needs. However, when she started to unpack and looking at my home as a kind of nest that needed maybe, a twig here a feather there, I could see her eyes penetrating the walls telling her a little more of the story of the man she had just recently married.

I was in a conflict over two aspects of myself. First of all, I wanted to get back into immersing myself in my work, putting in those incredibly long hours, utilizing my skills to their fullest possible degree, and becoming rich. On the other hand, I wanted to linger over drinks and dinner, just consuming my new wife and getting to know every little nook and cranny resting behind those baby blues.As we were beginning to lear our own particular roles in the husband-and-wife game, I was called to visit an important Corporate Client in Montreal. It would be about a two week trip, and as i always like to drive to "La Bell Provence", it was something I was quite looking forward to. The only problem was that I didn't want to be away from Marnie for such a long time, certainly not so soon after being wed. Marnie, with an eager smile and glint in her eyes, said, "you go and do what you have to do

I'll stay home and practice my housekeeping skills." I suggested that she joined me for a weekend, but she insisted that she wanted to stay at home. You sometimes just me for a weekend, but she insisted that she wanted to stay at home. you sometimes just have to accept your partners wishes, even though you may think your own ideas are better. I bundled up my best cloths in my new honeymoon suitcase , gassed up the Rolls, and was off. Every day, usually after dinner and drinks with with my client, I would phone home, eager to hear that soft, yet strong  voice, always reassuring me that everything was fine.

After my first two weeks separated from my loved ones, I was eager to get back home, to see her magnificent stature, her insightful glare, her soft yet determined voice, and to wrap my arms around the whole package. I arrived at the house fairly late on sunday evening, having driven about eight hours straight, stopping only to gas up and pee. I couldn't place it at first, but something seemed unsettling, the common seemed uncommon. Maybe it was just the fact that there was someone at home to greet me after two torturous weeks being consumed by corporate whims and fancy.

I wrestled with my key in the front door lock, and when the door opened, Marnie was there... I said. "What a surprise!" She replied, somewhat cryptically, "Yes, surprise number two." I'm afraid my head tilted to one side, much the way a dog's head will tilt when you say something it is alerted to. "Come in, come in," she encouraged, "and tell me what you think."

My house, once so austere, befitting a workaholic who spent so little time there, was now a home. Discrete lighting had been displaced by fluorescent tubing, brightening things considerably. Colourful, fluffy pillows had been covered in intricately designed Persian Carpets, there were intriguing intriguing painting hanging on the walls, and flowers everywhere. No longer did my house seem so practical and utilitarian. It was if Marnie had placed a welcome mat at my front door, and I had to agree completely with her interior design sensibility. It did feel more at home, comfortable surroundings coupled with the only person who I would have liked to have spent the rest of my life with, greeting me in a way that said that two weeks was way too long to have been away. With Marnie waiting waiting to greet me from the depths of heart at night, and a colourfull, cheerful home to spend time with her, my days become just that little bit shorter, and all of a sudden my primary goal was not to be the wealthiest person on Park Lane, but to be a nurturing and caring and loving husband. It became more important to spend time at home, rather than to be work.

The fact that Marnie had transformed my house into a home was good in and of itself, but it was also the type of thing I would have done if i were to make my house more homey. She just happened to understand my sensibilities and needs, as she would explain by saying that she could see it in my eyes. Life is not one long honeymoon... there are benalities and the mundane lurking behind this corner and that. The more you identify and spot the idiosyncrasies and particular traits of your partner, the more you step into the realm of the commonplace. That is both an advantage and a disadvantage. The first can be compared to staying at a Holiday Inn... you are tired after a busy day, and want to rest in a standard hotel room without any unwanted surprises. On the other hand, when you are on the road, you don't want to see just the ordinary or the commonplace, you want to see some thing or occurrence or place that will captivate your imagination and make the trip worthwhile and interesting. The thing that made Marnie as far from commonplace as could be was the fact that she really did know how to read people by looking in their eyes. There were no half measures possible, no white lies, and although she could surprise me on occasion (seven times, to be exact), I could never surprise her. Occasionally her perceptions were one step beyond what even I was aware of at the time. That certainly kept life interesting.

I was still intent on paying the mortgage, gassing the Rolls, and keeping the refrigerator stocked, but I was spending more time at home, primarily because the most wonderful person in my life lived there to, as well as the fact that Marnie had transformed my house into an abode that you just couldn't help but kick off the shoes and settle into a rather pleasant evening. I made a point of reserving Saturday nights and Sundays to spend with Marnie... On Saturday nights we would go out on the town, enjoying a concert, a movie, or a dramatic performance. On Sundays, Marnie would ask over a neighbor or two, and we would indulge in drink and encouraging debate, and when our guests would leave, Marnie would spend time cooking in the kitchen and would prepare a feast fit for kings. It was no coincidence that my first impression of her was that of a plate. But occasionally, there was more to theses Saturday nights and Sundays than one would expect.

Robert Munroe

One Saturday evening we were preparing to indulge in dinner and a dance at one of our favorite clubs downtown, when she said, "Wait for me downstairs... I won;t be long." I thought nothing of it, so I trundled downstairs and settled into an easy chair with the latest issue of Time Magazine. She took a little more time then i thought was necessary to get dressed, and i was just about to call to see if everything was okay, when she descended the stairs. She carried herself as if she were a leading a lady making a grand entrance. But where were her clothes? She was dressed in a see through blouse (and one could truly see through), a skirt that was notoriously short for the time, garter stockings and Stiletto heels. All of a sudden, I didn't want to go out for the evening... I wanted to go straight to bed. The thing was that Marnie usually wore polyester pants, sweatshirts and running shoes throughout the house, she did not have a very nice closet of clothes reeking of exotic prices, so she could dress up for occasions. I commented that people would not only look, but talk as well. She said, "that's the whole point... every other man can look, but I'm all for you only.

I was stimulated by what could only be called a costume, and I was aware of other men staring, eyes burning, and Marnie reading them as only she could. She called her dress (or undress) as surprise number three, and I enjoyed it immensely. I forgot about it shortly after... ocassionaly an image of this seductress would flash across my mind, but the second time she dressed in nearly nothing, i was completely taken by surprise again. After all, if she dressed so provocatively every Saturday night, it wouldn't be a surprise, or if it were, it would be a generic surprise. So I would never know when she would dress to turn heads, and she did this only on occasion, so that I would be completely taken aback when she did.

I always made a point of being with Marnie on Sundays. Regardless of whether we entertain guests in the afternoon, she would always have a substantial meal prepared for dinner. One night, after slaving i the kitchen one hot summer afternoon, I set the table. She wanted me out of the kitchen, and my enquires as to what was for dinner were met only by a smile. Eventually she declared that dinner was served, and she entered the dining room with plates covered with silver platters. She lifted the lid off my plate (much as what would be done in an upscale restaurant), and i couldn't identify the meat, and there were what looked like exotic chinese vegatbles. "What in the world is that?" I enquired. She just said, "try it and see."

The meat was tender an soft, a little bit salty, and altogether unrecognizable. It was rather tasty, and after chewing two mouthfuls, I said, "I give up. What is it?" She replied that it was penguin. I had to chuckle. It was like nothing I had eaten before. "Where in the world did you get penguin meat?" I enquired. "I have my sources," she said, and all i could picture was a contraband being brought into Toronto from Antarctica via some underground route. I slowly dawned on me that this was surprise number four., and just as in her erotic fashion sense, she would prepare some exotic dish, and then hamburgers or roast beef or fish, and just as i would get used to and expect similar and more common fare, she would bring out the sterling plate covers, and smile as she set the plates on the table. Nothing was too exotic, and nothing could I identify by sight or taste alone.

One night it would be narwhal, another it would be porpoise, around Christmas it would be reindeer. There would be nights of bison or buffalo, alligator or crocodile (there is a distinct difference in the taste between the two). I enjoyed the Yak, but the Elephant was a bit too tough. Chimpanzee steaks were rather tasty, but my favorite dinner was hippopotamus. I don't know were one would find recipe books on how to cook such dishes, but they were always cooked to perfection, sometimes with sauces or gravies, other times mixed in with pasta, or as part of a salad with ingredients from gosh knows what area of the world. I would always be the guinea pig, and be the one to take the first bite. We actually never ate guinea pig, but the rabbit good the couple times it was dished up.

Life with Marnie was not always a surprise. She no longer asked as many questions... I guess she was figuring out answers on her own. She still would pierce my eyes with her gaze on the odd occasion, but again, as we moved on in age, again she had seen much, or most of what there was to be seen. I knew her every bump and curve, I appreciate her sense of humour, I saw into her soul with more and more acumen. Things weren't always as delightful as I may seem to suggest, but we were comfortable and supportive with each other, and progressed with an easy pace.

Our sex life was good, particularly when Marnie would dress as provocatively as she could those rare Saturday nights, but I think the need for more and more caressing and intercourse dwindles somewhat the older you get. It is still an important part of any relationship between a man and a woman. We had discussed the possibility of having children, but we basically carried on as things were, not really waiting to change the structure of the family for the time being

I was always the first one out of bed, preferring to beat the traffic and get down to work early. One morning Marnie was up before I was. I could hear her vomiting violently into the toilet. I asked her if she was alright, and she replied that she probably had the twenty-four hour flu. I made her a pot of herbal tea, which should have settled her stomach and prevented dehydration. She was feeling somewhat better when I arrived home later that day,but was vomiting again before I was up the next day. "You probably have some sort of stomach virus,: i suggested, "maybe you should make an appointment to see Dr. Brett." "I'll wait one more day just in case it will go away on its own." Well, it didn't go away, so she made an appointment to see our doctor.

I arrived home a little earlier that day, eager to hear if Marnie had a simple virus, or something we should be more concerned about. "Surprise number five," she said. She was beaming from ear to ear. "What is it?" I asked. "I hope it's nothing too serious." "I'm due in four months." "Due what," I asked, puzzled. "I'm going to have a baby." As it turns out, Marnie had been five months pregnant, but in a one in a million case, her menstrual period never stopped. her vomiting had been a simple case of morning sickness.

The miraculous event a birth is gave our relationship new twists and turns. We were going to name the baby "Surrey," a form of work for surprise. First there were gurgles and diaper changing and feeding every two hours, a hungry mouth at any time of day or night. We kept a journal regarding the growth and development of our sweet little baby, astonished by each new word, tooth, sign of interests or destiny. As Surrey (a boy) grew older, he would play Marnie against me... "Mommy says I can go out to play." "No, you can't... You've been out for a while and you don't want to get a cold." One of his earliest passions was to play with finger paints or draw with crayons. Surrey definitely had a flare early on for art, and I always took it as not only an innate talent, but also a form of rebellion towards me, a numbers man.

Marnie was a great mother, able as always to see into the soul of her child. I was working a little less... I didn't want to miss seeing my son grow up. There were so many holidays to family entertainment, there was homework to help with, there were the birds and the bees to elaborate on, there were a multitude of experiences to share, so that Surrey's development was well rounded and he had many choices and options to pick between. Being an initial Surprise himself, he was, as Art Linklater would say on the black and white tv show, "saying the darndest things." It is natural for a child to Surprise, or cause joy or dismay just by the way he learns to look at the world and begin to make sense of it. I think that it also had to do with the fact that his mother was a great one for surprises, seven to be exact. surprises keep you on your toes and help keep life interesting. Marnie had done this all along, and now a child's innocence and curiosity was providing further fascination for my world and outlook. I would study Surrey's art work as a way of looking into his soul to see where his mind was at. I know Marnie was helpful and encouraging with her son, and I'd like to think I had a positive impact on his growth and development as well.

As Surrey grew older, Marnie and I advanced into middle age. Our focus in the middle of our relationship was largely directed at our son, and when he went off to art school in Manhattan, husband and wife were left to discover new dimensions in our relationship. So much of our life had become familiar and mundane that we could often communicate without speaking, letting an offhand gesture or glint in the eye, say everything. When a man grows older he becomes more comfortable with himself. When a woman grows older, the initial attraction of her physique diminishes and there are wrinkles and sagging and sunspots. Motherhood is the next stage, where you just want to share in the raising of your child, consulting over better or worse ways of doing so. In the third stage, the initial attraction and then the role of motherhood are left behind, and the only alternative is to become more cultured and interesting. Marnie ploughed into this pursuit with the gusto she had applied to me, herself, and her son.

I came home one night, and Marnie came out with the words unexpectedly, "I've signed up for a couple courses." I was expecting something like knitting or crocheting, but she only said, "no, silly, one is on ancient Mayan history, and the other one is on the Russian Revolution. Then, when I'm finished with those, I'm going to take a course in photography." "Well that's a Surprise. Good for you." It wasn't long before Marnie would be peppering our dinner conversations with talk of Rasputin and Czars and Feudalism and Communism, followed by the dimensions of the pyramids of Macchu Picchu and how the Incas would tell time. I soon came to find out that this kindling of her creative and intellectual outlets would be surprise number six. She would converse with me about remote and far away times and places, her passion and eloquence inspiring and captivating my imagination. Eventually, a couple of paintings on the walls were taken down, and landscape photos and dozens of versions of my profile were erected in their place.

One night, when we were in bed, not as hot and bothered as we once were, i caressed her breasts, and felt a little lump or bump on the underside of the left one. I asked Marnie if she was aware of this. She said she had noticed it a couple weeks previously, but thought nothing of it. I gave her the statistic for women who develop breast cancer, and she suggested she go see Dr. Brett, who had been there for us right from the beginning. Dr. Brett sent Marnie for a biopsy, and praised her decision to be examined. As it turns out, the lump was malignant. Dr. Brett was very cautious and thorough in sharing with us what to expect. We eventually agreed that the breast should be removed, and that things would be alright after that. As it happened, the malignancy was much more advanced then we had hoped or expected. I took some time off my Accountancy practice, and cared for and supported Marnie through what was perhaps the most difficult time of her life. She wanted to stay at home, and for a while, short visits to the hospital for Chemotherapy seemed to be satisfactory. Instead of getting better, however, things took a turn for the worse, and I called to bring Surrey home to spend the final couple of weeks left that his mother, my wife, would live.

A large contingency of Marnie's family and friends arrived
from Winnipeg for the funeral, and what with her friends and
neighbours in Toronto, it was a send-off fit for a queen. Then
came the crunch. I felt lost without Marnie. I would go back
to my younger schedule of long hours at work, trying to keep
my mind off my grief, but my grief was always there taunting
and tormenting me. I talked to Surrey every day to offer him
my support and claim the same from him. The house was still
empty when I came home each evening, and the manner in
which Marnie had arranged and decorated our house was
just another painful reminder that she was no longer waiting
for me at home at the end of the day. I felt only half myself
when i lay in bed for countless sleepless hours every night.
Mostly, I desired to have her look into my eyes, knowing that
she could see all I was, and accepting me with my successes
and failures, my ups and downs, my good points as well as
the less desirable ones. And I thought about her surprises,
and wondered if she had foreseen her own death, and the last
Surprise was that she would leave me when we were both
still in the prime of our lives. I was soon to find that that was
not the case.

Christmas was always a wonderful time at the household.
Marnie would start her shopping in the middle of June,
would serve countless feasts to friends and neighbours,
would bake countless pies and cakes, and entertain as often
as she could. Surrey was due home for Christmas. I had not
been much in the spirit of the season, and had not decorated
the house, nor gone shopping, nor had I entertained. There
was no way in the world I could have done Marnies efforts

justice. I sent out no cards, as I figured that everyone who should know about the passing of Marnie would already know. It is also hard to be jolly with season's greetings when you hurt inside so much. Christmas was a time of year to suffer through, when you are acutely aware of your loss.

The neighbours were very good at entertaining Surrey and I, understanding that reaching out to others while in pain is difficult to do. They were great. Then, an unusual thing happened. A letter arrived from Marnie, but it was addressed in her maiden name. I thought it may have been an old advertisement, but the envelope was handwritten. I was intrigued, and it was the first piece of mail I opened that day. It read as follows:

Ralph Thyme
#33 Coutts Lane
Lankashire, U.K.
V6B AAKL

My Dear Marnie:

I didn't hear from you this year, and hope things are alright. I think of our correspondence over the past thirty years, and was concerned not to get any word from you. That brief two months we spent in London on your whirlwind trip had sustained me over the ensuing decades, I remember an incredible sight as you sat at Cromwell's Tea House, so long ago, and how you came over and asked for the directions to the Tower of London.
I remember your curiosity and insightful gaze with those baby blues. And those surprises you could see long before they happened. I can remember your caresses and sweet

kisses; time has not dulled my memory of you in the least. You aroused my passions, and I wonder how you could never share that love with someone for the rest of your life. I was thankful for the two months we spent together, that was not enough, but enough to sustain me for a lifetime.

You are so superb at reading people and getting them to open up to you, but i feel somewhat perplexed that you never reveal anything of yourself. Please come over one more time... I never saw London in quite the same way as I did when I was with you. There have been so many changes over the decades and so much more to see. I never married. My memory of you was branded in my brain so that no other woman could be compared with you on an equal basis.

I am thinking of selling the family business and spending through winters in the south of Spain or maybe Gibraltar. Life is to short not to do something nice for yourself on occasion. Won't you accept my offer of a winter in the south? Please write as soon as possible. I am eager to hear your news.

Love,
Ralph Thyme

It all of a sudden struck me that this unknown friend/suitor was the final Surprise, in my life, not Marnie's premature death. And I could be pretty well certain that I would be the final surprise of many for Mr. Thyme. But I had to wonder how Marnie could carry on three decades of correspondence without revealing anything about me, Surrey, or her interests, pursuits, or surprises. I immediately put pen to paper.

Gregory Jantis
661 Park Lane
Toronto, Ont.
Canada
M4V 6D6

Dear Mr. Thyme:

No doubt this letter will come as a complete surprise
to you. I am the widower of Marnie McMillan. I had no idea
you were carry on a correspondence with Marnie after a filing
of some three decades ago. When I first met her, at a neighbourhood party, she claimed I would have seven major surprises in my life. The first one was that I would get married,
and this was a surprise indeed, as I was a committed workaholic bachelor. The last one, as i see it, is that Marnie had a
friend for so long, and I had no such clue whatsoever that
you were in the picture.

I was enamored of Marnie right from the first time I
saw her, and attraction became full blown love shortly after. I
could see how you could never marry after having the experience of knowing Marnie for a brief two months years ago.

She was a wonderful companion, always giving more
then she took. We raised a son who is currently at Art
School in Manhattan, and she kept life interesting by surprising me with food, dress, a child, educational pursuits, and
finally you.

I am a man of means, and took care of your friend the
best I could. She ment the world to me, and the darkness of
my bereavement is occasionally illuminated by some wonderful memory or another of our life together. I am intrigued that
you would be somewhere in the picture of her life, but i have

one question... what in the world did she correspond with
you about when my life, my son's life, our family goings on,
were not mentioned?

Yours,
Geoffrey Jantis

I sent a copy of Mr. Thymes letter to Surrey, and he was not
only surprised but pleased. "Leave it to mom to surprise us
once more after her death."

A letter was prompt in arriving for Mr. Thyme:

Ralph Thyme
#33 Coutts Lane
Lankashire, U.K.
V6B AAKL

Dear Mr. Jantis:

It was indeed a surprise to hear from you, the widower of a
friend of mine that goes back some thirty years. As you cor-
rectly guessed, I was completely unaware of your existence. I
am sad at the passing of a good friend, but also delighted that
she was well taken care of and performed her duties as a
mother and wife, as every woman is destined to, biologically.
My memory of your wife is heightened even in her death.

As for what we correspond about, well, just as we had done
together in London so many years ago, she would take me on
a tour of Toronto through her letters. It was as if she was my
own tour guide, albeit from a distance. I feel that I have an
intimate understanding of the sights and sounds and smells
of your fair city, thanks to her.

Yes, she did ask a lot of questions, and talked about surprises. It was as if she was enveloped in a sea of fog, and the only way to remover herself from the thick pea soup was to question politely but relentlessly what I (and no doubt you) saw. By asking questions, not only did she have a more complete picture of the world, but I felt as if I understood the world more, myself.

Congratulations for having the most amazing woman in the world, my friend, as your wife. I am sure she made you very happy. What the heck... I'll extend my invitation for a trip to Spain to you, too! Make sure to bring photos and mementoes if you come.

Sincerely,
Ralph Thyme

In Christian faith, Christmas is a time of faith and hope. Hearing from Mr. Thyme in a way brought Marnie back to me, seeing a sign that things about her life that were entirely new, and hopeful. Clearly the seventh surprise was the biggest one of all. But I had no need to tell Marnie that.

# Lunar Shadows Cast
# Upon A Midnight Crisis

BUZZ. That damn phone. It was either Sally calling from
Saskatoon, or Mr. Jenkins wanting me in his office right away.
The move and promotion had brought about a lot of change
in my life., and I felt just enough off balance to find them
unsettling. The buzz of the phone ment that something had
gone wrong somewhere. For the past two weeks, whenever
the phone buzzed, I had come to expect difficulty on the
other end.

Saskatoon is a nice, average, small to mid-sized city situated
on the prairies. It is cold as hell in the winter time, but everyone makes up for it by thriving on the short summers. There
doesn't seem to be any spring or fall. One minute your shiver-
ing, and the next moment your sweating. I grew up in a small
town on the prairies, so small I wont even bother to mention
it's name. So when I moved to Saskatoon, it was kind of like
moving to the center of things, the bright lights of the big city.
I used my high school accounting skills to get a job doing the
books at Wenkel Automotive Supplies, the local outfit of a
national chain of performance car supplies and accessories. I
found the company more interesting then the job I was doing,
but I was employed gainfully and making more then a modest living, so I was happy.

Everyone knows everyone else's business i a small town. A
routine develops that is both cozy and familiar. However, in
Saskatoon, there was so much to discover. Theatres, live the-
atre, cafes, restaurants, live music, bookstores, music shops,
and of course the library, where one could look up information on anything. And of course, news happened in
Saskatoon. Things of substance took place that people read
about across Canada. But it was the women that really struck

my fancy. There is nothing more wholesome then a farm bred girl, but there were women in Saskatoon. Smart blouses, short skirts, panty hose and high heels. High fashion, punkers, the University type, the hippy, the office worker, the mother, the athlete. Coming from a small town, one couldn't help but take notice of how fashion was used to make a statement by women. And I couldn't help but listen to what was being said, or should I say look. I felt like a kid in a candy shop, and couldn't help but reach into the bin.

Wenkel's was in an industrial park on the rim of town. All around us were strip malls and small factories and car dealerships and transport trucks. It was the kind of place where you arrived just before starting time in the morning, and didn't linger when it was time to go home at the end of the day. About the only time I wasn't travelling to or from work in the area, was at lunch. That was when I would go to Ed's Grill. There were a couple of other places in the neighbourhood where one could lunch, but they were all so generic and geared to getting you in and out in seven and a half minutes or less. Ed's was like a museum piece from the fifties. First of all, you knew it was a good place because there were always several big rigs idling in the vast parking lot out front. It was built so that it resembled a gas station, with bay doors that let in a lot of light. Inside, there was a long counter stretching from one end of the building around a corner to the other side. The tables were also formica counters, and the actual grill itself was all stainless steel. More often then not, I would spend my lunch hours here.

I liked to sit at a table by one of the large roll up bay doors, and watch the traffic roll by. I would have my hamburger or fish and chips or chicken nugget's, and down it with a large tumbler full of coke. Then I would take in the din of constant chatter above the piped in music, and watch the waitresses and kitchen staff hustle their buns for the noon rush. I soon had my favorite table, and I would leave the office a little early so that I would be assured my table wasn't taken. And with a regular table came a regular waitress. She appeared to be about my age, about 22, her name tag told me her name was Sally. She was dressed in a white men's shirt, black dress pants, running shoes and had a money pouch around her waist. She was always prompt. One day I was asked to stay over lunch at work to get something done right away, and wasn't able to get to Ed's until about 1:30. The place had thinned out considerably at this time from the usual noon rush. Sally came over right away.

"I see you're eating fashionably late today."

"I had to stay and finish some work. Rush job."

"Where do you work? That is if you don't mind me asking. I serve you so often, I almost feel as if i know you already."

"I work down the block at Wenkel's. You know, hot rod accessories. I do the books there."

"I was going to say, you don't strike me as the grease monkey type."

"It's a job."

"Yeah, me too. I just finished my degree at the university, and waitressing is tiding me over until something better comes along."

"Look at it this way. You're providing sustenance for these people. There's nothing more basic nor essential then that. What did you study?

"Sociology, I don't know what good it's going to do for me. But I have a degree. That's the main thing."

"That's more then what I can say.What would you like to do?"

"Oh, I don't know. Maybe move to Regina and work for the provincial government. I want something that has security."

"You're not taking the traditional route of a husband and two kids and a white picket fence?"

"Maybe eventually, but I don't want to settle down jus⁻ yet. I'm still too young. There are still too many things I want to do."

I took this as a cue. "How would you like to go see the new Blake Rodriguez movie playing at the Odeon tonight?"

"Well.... okay. Come around at 7:30. That's when i get off work. Then we can catch a bite to eat before the flick. I've been dying to see it."

"Okay, 7:30 it is. Have you seen Rodriguez's other movies?"

"Most of them. We already have something in common, it seems.:

"Well, after the movie, if you're up to it, maybe we can go to the By the Whey Cafe and see what else we have in common."

"Everyone else that eats in here eats in here either turns a screw or drives a truck. It's nice to meet someone like you here. I'll see you at 7:30 tonight then."

I watched her trim figure with small petit breasts and a long ponytail trailing behind as she receded into the kitchen behind swinging doors, and I was so enthralled by the fact that I had a date with this woman, that it took me a minute to realize that she never took my order. She came back giggling a couple minutes later and apologized for the oversight. As I had my lunch, I took special notice of Sally as she traversed Ed's. She was as graceful and quick as a gazelle.

The movie lived up to our expectations, and the drinks we had afterwards enabled us to discover many things we had in common. It was a late night, and I had trouble getting up for work the next day. The morning went slowly, as i anxiously waited for lunch time to roll by. Sally was pretty busy, so she didn't have a lot of time to talk, but she did say how much she enjoyed the evening, and would like to do it again sometime.

I asked for and received permission to take my lunch later in the afternoon. This enabled me to catch Sally when she wasn't so busy, and she would have a little time to spare to chat. So every day I would enter Ed's at about 1:30 and have a bit of a chat with Sally as I ordered my lunch. On Friday or Saturday nights we would hit the town and would enjoy some performance or outing. These occasions became more and more frequent, until about the only time we weren't seeing each other was during working hours. So we did the most natural thing and she moved into my apartment.

We would catch up with each other after work at the

apartment, and go grocery shopping a couple times a week. each time buying food with more and more outrageous recipes in mind. Then he would prepare dinner, sometimes taking turns and surprising each other, but often cooking together. Then we would sit on the couch and watch television or read to each other or play board games or do crossword puzzles. Sometimes we would talk... for hours at a time. And occasionally we would visit a nightclub or see a movie. But we would always go to bed early so that we could make wild, passionate love.

At the same time my love life was looking up, my job was looking up as well. I had become adept and efficient at handling the books, and was given additional work which brought about a higher salary. I was respected by my coworkers and appreciated by my boss. The better I became and the more I was appreciated, the more I put into my work. It became a marvelously viscous circle. The boss started hinting at a promotion. I started thinking about furnishing my apartment a little better.

Sally was there to charge in my growing good fortune. But in some ways I felt bad because she was not getting any further with her career moves. She was still hustling her butt for basic wages and tips during the lunch and dinner rush at Ed's. Meanwhile, I was getting a larger salary and greater responsibility and more respect and additional considerations. But she kept on saying her time would come. AS it happened, the timing wasn't right.

One day, just before lunch and my chance to say hi to Sally, the head honcho at Wenkel's called me into his office. He had me take a seat, shut the door, and buzzed the secretary to hold all calls for a few moments.

"Keith, how are you doing?"

"Fine, Sir."

"That's good. I'm pleased to hear that. I want you to know that we're very pleased with you. You are hard working and industrious and efficient, and seem to care for the well being of the company. That hasn't gone unnoticed. Fortunately that puts you in a good bargaining position. You can write your own ticket. And a Ticket has come your way for Toronto. A position has just opened up in Toronto, that is right up your alley. It would be more then a bit of a promotion for you, with a sizable increase in salary. All of your moving expenses and relocating fees will be paid for by Wenkel's. I have recommended you for the position as we want to have an internal candidate chosen first, and you are the prime choice. We see you going far. Now I have the proposal here that I want you to read over carefully before you make any decision. It's a major decision to make, something that could change your life potentially, so I want you to take your time thinking it over."

"Thank you Sir, I appreciate the consideration. I'll think it over carefully."

"We need you here, Keith, but you're needed even more in Toronto. So I hope you make the decision that will benefit you, and the company, the most."

With that, he got up and opened the door for me, giving me a smile and a wink as i passed him on my way out. At first I was overjoyed. Imagine, being considered for a major transfer to head office. The increase in pay. The added respect. Additional responsibility. Toronto, the center of the world, where all of the action takes place. I begin to see myself in a high-rise downtown, looking out onto the Skydome and the CN Tower, attending great cultural events and searching for the uncommon item in specialty stores. But then I had a change of heart. My job in Saskatoon was familiar and safe. And I knew what to expect and could react accordingly. I knew the city by now and had my favorite haunts. But most importantly, Sally was in Saskatoon. My best friend and lover. Would she, or could she, just pick up her things and leave Saskatoon behind with nothing to go to? I couldn't afford to pay her way. I was a bit confused by the opportunity.

On this particular day, i took an early lunch. I wanted to break the news to Sally and hear what she had to say. I walked slowly over to Ed's and hesitated at the door, trying to formulate in my mind what i was going to say.

"You're early today. I'm rushed off my feet right now."

"I couldn't wait to come over and tell you."

"Tell me what?."

"I've been offered a transfer to Toronto."

"Well... that's... that's swell, isn't it?"

"It's a big promotion. That's for sure."

"What about us? Would you want me to come, too? I could always leave for Toronto when you get settled."

"Right now we both can't go to Toronto. It's just beyond the question. However, in time, you could come out and find a job. There may even be good opportunities for Sociologists. You could get out of the grind of waitressing."

"Yeah, I guess I'd have to save up some money before making the trip."

"It won't take too long."

"Well, I'll miss you when you first move. But as they say, when opportunity knocks..."

Over the course of the next week, I read the proposal several times, and contemplated my options. Sometimes you have to keep up with progress, and go with the sands of change. Also, a major opportunity had been dropped in my lap, and such luck might not come my way again. I thought again of Sally, and the fact that I couldn't afford to bring her with me... at least not right away. Would the relationship be the same after after an absence? Would there be other attractions with a new home base? I loved Sally, and I thought our relationship was firm, but it hadn't tested any major change. Would it stand the test of time and distance?

At the end of the week, I had made up my mind: I would go. I would take charge of my destiny and help make things happen. I would leave behind my beloved city of Saskatoon, and briefly leave behind Sally. I hoped that our absence from each other for even a short time would not damage the relationship. I tried to count my blessings and not focus on the negatives. Things would work out okay.

I sublet my apartment to Sally, and gave her the instructions that she was to sell everything when she followed me up east. I was starting anew in Toronto. I could afford to. Wenkel's put me up in an apartment hotel for two months while looked at vacancies after work. I found a nice flat in the Annex area of the city, near the University, and where all kinds of things were happening. It ment that I had to commute to Scarborough to the head office and warehouse of Wenkel's, but I liked my neighbourhood.

Coming originally from a small prairie town, and then Saskatoon, Toronto seemed so big. There were people and tall buildings and cars everywhere. And fast. Everyone moved at such a great clip. There's dynamics in Toronto. In my job in Saskatoon, I seemed to be the only competitive spirit around. In Toronto, EVERYONE is competitive, fighting and pushing for their rightful piece of the action. I just had to work all that much harder.

My life changed. I was in a new city, had a new apartment, and had new responsibilities. My circle of acquaintances was enlarging slowly, as well. But Sally was still in the same apartment, with my belongings, her same old job, in the same old city. For her, the status quo hadn't really changed all that much. For me, it had changed almost completely. The only thing that stayed the same for me were my memories. For this reason, Sally would call me at work once or twice a day, and usually once at night. They would be short calls. She usually didn't have any news. She just wanted to hear my voice, to be reassured that I was alright. The only other time the phone buzzed was when it was Mr. Jenkins.

Mr. Jenkins was my boss. He was an older gentleman,

waiting for his retirement. He was tall and in good shape for his age, and always impeccably dressed. But he was what you might call jocular. He would walk up to your desk and put his arm around your shoulder, and start talking about team-work and use football metaphores a lot. He had his own way of doing things, and everyone who worked under him had to conform to the same system. He was constantly calling me into his office to consult me on some small matter, or to point out how another way might work better. Since I was the new kid on the block, he made me his pet project.

So here I was, two weeks into the new job, and the phone was buzzing again. I had 50/50 odds of guessing who it would be. This time it turned out to be Mr. Jenkins. He called for me to come into his office. As usual, as i passed the water cooler, the triplets were there, chattering away. I guess if you ever wanted to know any juicy office gossip, they would be the ones to ask. And every-time they saw me, they'd break into titters. Did I smell or was I ugly? Did i appear to them as a martian? Then I passed Jim Plant's desk. He gave me a begrudging smile. I was chosen over him for the position I now hold. As I walked into Mr. Jenkin's office, Stacey Mindley came out. When I wasn't dreaming of Sally, I was lusting after Stacey. She was one hot looking chick. But she was always so cold and businesslike.

Mr. Jenkins sat me down in his office and explained that every year Wenkel's throws a midnight cruise party in Toronto Harbour for it's employees, and that these are great affairs that are talked about in the office for weeks after-wards. He said that it would be a great chance for me to get to know all my fellow workers and make some friends.

Would I like a ticket? I thought about the fact that it usually takes me a while to get to know people, and that I am no good at parties, and that on a cruise you just can't get up and leave if you're having a bad time, but I said yes because i felt like I had some kind of duty to the company to be present. I didn't want to get involved with office personalities and positions. I just wanted to my job and nothing else.

As the date of the cruise approached, I began to dread the whole affair. I would be under the close scrutiny of everyone on the ship, being the new kid on the block. Every word or phrase I spoke would be judged, every action preformed would be compared to others'. It wouldn't be like when I was with Sally, where you could let loose so to speak and bring down your guard. With Sally, anything was alright because it was a part of you. She made me feel good about myself. But the people at Wenkel's Toronto office were all stuck up fashion plates who were out for their own advancement at the cost of anyone else who might be standing nearby. I was worried about getting to know my fellow workers too well on the cruise.

I liked my new apartment and the city of Toronto, but i found learning the ropes of my new job a bit challenging, and my fellow workers a bit off putting. Mr. Jenkins kept calling me into his office to point out this or that. He was very meticulous. He kept me on my toes. Not having Sally around to engage in a little pillow talk, the sight of Stacey was quite tormenting. But I managed somehow, reminding myself that I was moving up in the world, and that this required greater and greater efforts to be put forth.

Robert Munroe

After work the night of the cruise I went home to get changed into something less formal. I had yet to see the harbour, so i figured that this was going to be a treat. After all, there are no large bodies of water in Saskatoon, just a river. I took a cab down to Pier 16, where The Toronto Princess was moored. The Toronto Princess was a blue and white ship that could hold about 100 people. There was a glassed in lower deck, where a buffet was set up. Up above, there was an open deck, complete with a bar, amid the station house where the captain drove the ship. Strung between poles on the upper deck were brightly coloured lanterns, which cast a rainbow glow into the night. A band was setting up its instruments on the lower deck when I arrived. I walked up a red carpeted gangplank into the hold of the ship, where I saw few familiar faces, and many unfamiliar ones, no doubt from the warehouse.

No sooner did I get a beer beer than that, I heard the winch of the gangplank and the hum of the engine, and as I leaned out an open porthole,I could hear the soft lapping of waves against the hull. One of the employees, John Gingham, was an amateur astronomer, and he pointed out the various constellations in the sky. It was amazing to see him make sense of the starry night. The night sky seemed like a canopy covering the earth. It seemed so immense.

I was on the lower deck enjoying a canapé when who should approach but Jim Plant. I was hoping to avoid him, for fear that he would hold a grudge for me taking the job away from him. But he was very nice. He said that he was glad that I got the job, that he had some doubts as to whether he could have done it.

He asked if I was into cars or whether this was just a job for
me. When I told him it was just a job, he said that that was
the case for him too. He liked working for Wenkels, it was a
good company to work for. But his passion was chess. I told
him that unfortunately I didn't play, and he offered to teach
me. I said that maybe when I got settled in a bit more I'd be
ready to learn. We started to talk about Mr. Jenkins, about
how he was a decent guy but a bit of a task master, when he
approached the canapés.

Mr. Jenkins was as dapperly dressed as ever, but he seemed a
bit more relaxed, not quite as comradery forced as when he
was at the office. He spoke about how Jim and I were such
fine, upstanding fellows, and that I was going to take over his
job some day. He slapped us both on the back at the same
time, almost dislodging a bit of canapé midway down my
throat. Shortly thereafter he wandered off and Jim and I
exchanged knowing glances. Mr.Jenkins could be seen down
the deck slapping the back of another employee and laughing
merrily. Jim saw someone he wanted to speak to, so he
excused himself.

I went to the bar to get another beer when who should I
encounter but the triplets. It was fitting that they should be
standing around a watering hole, much like they did constantly
at work. They were giggling as usual, but they seemed to be
keenly interested in me. They asked if I had a girlfriend or was
married, and I told them about Sally. Then they asked what it
was like on the prairies, and does it really get that cold in the
winter time? They didn't tell me that much about themselves, but
they knew me pretty well by the time I left them.

I figured everyone in the office would know just about everything about me by the time I got to work on Monday. But
with their giggles and wide eyed astonishment at everything
I said, they made it fun to talk.

I decided to go to the upper deck when the band started playing. I wanted to see the night sky again. Most of the people
were on the lower deck where the band and the bar and the
food was. On the upper deck was Stacey Findley. She was
dressed in a halter top, tight jean shorts that made her but-
tocks resemble a pear, and cork lace-up platform shoes. She
waltzed over to me when I came out of the stair well. She was
concerned for my wee being... being in a new city full of
strangers, in a new job, away from my girlfriend. She seemed
much more approachable on board the ship than she did, so
business-like at work.

At the sound of the first slow song, she wrapped her arms
around my neck and slowly we spun across the upper deck,
beneath the glistening stars. It had been a couple of weeks
since I had been with Sally, so that the attention and care
Stacey showed me was greatly appreciated. She seemed to
understand that I was lonely and needed the embrace of a
woman. It is amazing how much people can change once
they are out of the office environment.

The evening slowly stretched out ahead of us. The Toronto
Princess plowed through the waters of Lake Ontario, the lights of
the office buildings in the downtown core acted as a beacon for
the boat. I met about 100 people that night, some of whom I
would get to know fairly well over the upcoming months.

But mostly, I realized, I was introducing myself to my fellow workers. The effect of the ship the party atmosphere on board brought out a side of people that I hadn't seen at work. They seemed to be more of themselves and less as if they were playing a role or performing. When the boat came in to dock, I quickly swallowed one last canape and ran up to the upper deck to look out over the Harbor one last time. I looked up and could see a three-quarter moon casting its rays over the ship and overseeing the evenings events.

When I got home that night, I lay in my bed pondering the evenings events. My initial apprehensions proved unfounded, and I seem to have seen a different side of everyone. Especially Stacey. She made me realize how much I missed Sally. It was as if for the past couple weeks I had been living the fast paced, important life of a high executive, while at the same time for getting my roots in Sally, in whom I felt comfortable and at ease. I looked at my bedside clock. It said, quarter to three. I picked up the phone and dialed Sally. I had to tell her to come quick.

Robert Munroe

# The Bookcase

Robert Munroe

CPSIA information can be obtained at www.ICGtesting.com
Printed in the USA
242187LV00001B/10/P